CONSTANTINE
IS THE LITTLE HORN
OF DANIEL CHAPTER 7

By

Gary Wendell Stanfield Sr.

DEDICATION

I dedicate this book to those immersed in Christianity, unaware of how profoundly Satan deceives people, leading them to unknowingly embrace and perpetuate the falsehoods of Christianity through the principle of "say it enough, and they will believe it." This book is also for those earnestly seeking the truth, convinced that there must be something beyond what Christianity presents as the truth. This search for authenticity was my journey, prompting me to rigorously test everything I had been taught to discern its veracity. This book is the culmination of years of study, during which I have learned far more than what these pages contain, necessitating follow-up books.

When I began my journey, I was in a similar position as you might be now, feeling lost and uncertain about the path to salvation. You, too, may have struggled to find any truth despite extensive study, unsure of where to turn or what steps to take next. Understanding that Christianity doesn't hold the answers, yet yearning to know what truly offers salvation can be daunting. This book aims to guide you to that truth, unlocking doors to genuine salvation and shedding light on many other teachings found in the scriptures.

PREFACE

Matthew 16: 2-3

²*He answered and said unto them, When it is evening, ye say, It will be fair weather: for the sky is red. ³And in the morning, It will be foul weather today: for the sky is red and lowering. O ye hypocrites, ye can discern the face of the sky; but can ye not discern the signs of the times?*

"CONSTANTINE IS THE LITTLE HORN OF DANIEL CHAPTER 7."

Studies done by Gary Wendell Stanfield Sr.

All poems written by Gary W. Stanfield Sr.

Table of Contents

CHAPTER 1
NIMROD TO CONSTANTINE

NIMROD AND CONSTANTINE

It was Emperor Constantine who started Christianity.

He had changed Yahweh's Word, which was insanity.

Just so he could deceive the world and all humanity.

This was done for control and for his own self-vanity.

Nimrod and Constantine are two of the same,

To deceive humanity was their whole game.

This is why both are fully to blame,

And why they both will burn in the flame.

Constantine's vision of the Cross he would sell,

So in Nimrod's paganism, humanity would dwell.

If Christians knew the truth surely, they would yell,

Because, in their beliefs, they would all go to hell.

This Babylonian religion will be destroyed by the King,

Yahweh Messiah to Him believers will securely cling.

That is when His people, a new song they will sing,

When Yahweh ends this Babylonian religious thing.

By Gary W. Stanfield Sr.

To know where Constantine's pagan belief system came from, you must start with Nimrod with the First Seal. NIMROD STARTED PAGAN SUN WORSHIP, WITH HIM AS THE SUN, SOL WAS THE OLDEST NAME FOR HIM AS THE SUN AND CONSTANTINE WORSHIPED THE SUN AS SOL. Nimrod was the first Pontifex Maximus (Pope).

FALSE MESSIAH AND KING (1ST SEAL)

Nimrod was given the first kingdom on Earth,

He was the one who gave paganism its birth.

A deity he became to lead the world astray,

So that man would worship him and not Yahweh.

Nimrod defied Yahweh by building a tower,

Yahweh came down with His mighty power,

Giving different languages to spoil Nimrod's plan,

Along with the languages, the scattering of man.

The "Tower of Babel" is what it became known,

Another reason Nimrod lost his throne.

Nimrod, the first false messiah and king,

Thus, eternal death to himself he did bring.

This Babylonian religious system will see its end,

When Yahweh and His Messengers all descend,

To wipe the people out who did not believe in Him,

And the armies that go against Zion, known as Jerusalem.

By Gary W. Stanfield Sr.

Nimrod not only being the first Pontifex Maximus/Pope, but I believe he will also be the last one. He is also the founder of Assyria.

Daniel 11:37 *He shall regard neither the deity of his fathers nor the desire of women, nor regard any deity; for he shall exalt himself above them all.*

2 Thessalonians 2:4 *Who opposeth and exalteth himself above all that is called deity, or that is worshipped; so that he as deity sitteth in the temple of God, shewing himself that he is a deity.*

He will literally sit in the Temple of God and not the House of Yahweh that they replaced with the word "Temple." Temples were used by sun worshipers.

Daniel 8:23-25

23 And in the latter time of their kingdom, when the transgressors come to the full, a king of fierce countenance and understanding dark sentences shall stand up.

24 And his power shall be mighty, but not by his own power: and he shall destroy wonderfully, and shall prosper, and practice, and shall destroy the mighty and the righteous people.

25 And through his policy also he shall cause craft to prosper in his hand; and he shall magnify himself in his heart, and by peace shall destroy many: he shall also stand up against the King of Kings; but he shall be broken without hand.

In the above verse, *"King of Kings"* was replaced by *"Prince of Princes,"* A king is over a prince, so Yahweh Messiah is King of Kings.

I believe Nimrod will be brought back to be the last Pope since he understands dark sentences and he was the one that turned his back on Yahweh. He did not regard Yahweh of his fathers and he was an

Assyrian, a Pope can come from any country now. Nimrod was also the first Pontifex Maximus; and he was the one who started pagan religions.

<u>Assyria was a kingdom in northern Mesopotamia, located in what is now northern Iraq and southeastern Turkey</u>. <u>Its capital was Nineveh, which is now Mosul, Iraq</u>.

Today, the region of Assyria is divided among Iraq, Syria, Turkey, and Iran, and a sense of Assyrian identity has resurfaced among some people living in these countries

Isaiah 10:5,12

5 O Assyrian, the rod of mine anger, and the staff in their hand is my indignation.

12 Wherefore it shall come to pass, that when Yahweh hath performed his whole work upon mount Zion, I will punish the fruit of the stout heart of the king of Assyria and the glory of his high looks.

Isaiah 14:25: *"That I will break the Assyrian in my land, and upon my mountains tread him under foot: then shall his yoke depart from off them, and his burden depart from off their shoulders."*

Micah 5:6 And they shall waste the land of Assyria with the sword, and the land of Nimrod in the entrances thereof: thus shall he deliver us from the Assyrian, when he cometh into our land, and when he treadeth within our borders.

Nimrod created new cities, and one of them was Asshur, which became Assyria.

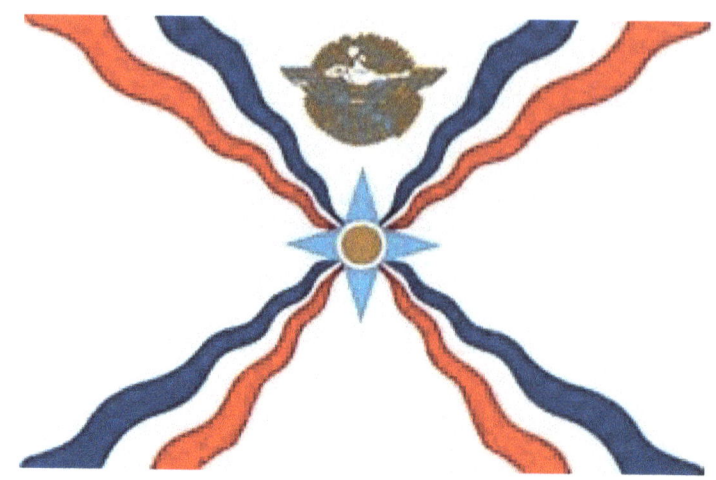

The Assyrian flag - three waving stripes emerge from each corner of a center design, which is in the shape of a four-headed star. At its center, the star encompasses a golden circle representing Shamash, the Assyrian sun deity. Shamash is Nimrod in his pagan sun worship. Shamash, Assyrians believed it gave life to all things on earth. The four wedges of the star are a bright blue color and represent happiness and tranquility. The blue represents the Euphrates River, the white represents the Great Zab River, and the red represents the Tigris River; wavy Stripes symbolize the three major rivers flowing through the land of Assyria. The emblem of Ashur features the deity standing in a circle with two eagle wings spanning and stretching its length on two sides.

Ashur has drawn a bow; I see no arrow, just like the description of Nimrod in the first Seal that represents him. Ashur is also another name for Nimrod, a sun deity. In the worship of Nimrod, he began to enslave men for his kingdom, and he decided to have them build a tower to the heavens. Nimrod started slavery with his own relatives. Nimrod, who was a mighty hunter and ruler on the Earth. He was the son of Cush, and his grandfather was Noah's son Ham.

FIRST SEAL - BABYLONIAN EMPIRE - WHITE HORSE

All of the following represent the Babylonian Empire

1. Head of Gold = Babylonian Empire - Daniel 2:38
2. Lion with Wings = Babylonian Empire - Daniel 7:4
3. Mouth of a Lion - Babylonian Empire - Revelation 13:2
4. RIDER ON WHITE HORSE- BABYLONIAN EMPIRE - Revelation 6:2

This WHITE HORSE represents FALSE MESSIAH.

Nimrod is the White Horse rider with the crown and bow. Nimrod the Assyrian.

He represents the Babylonian Empire, which I will prove. He, by conquest, was given the first kingdom on Earth. The first false messiah by paganism, he gave birth.

Nimrod came in his own name, and the world received him.

John 5:43 I have come in my Father's name, and ye receive me not: if another shall come in his own name, him ye will receive.

The Church of God is now teaching that it is Nimrod who is the rider on this White Horse; their video is no longer on YouTube, which they did not teach before. They are teaching, though, that the White Horse represents a counterfeit Christianity, but all Christianity is a lie and farce. Yet they teach the other horses that Christianity has always taught them to be, like when I was growing up, which is not true.

Who does this represent?

Genesis 10:8 And Cush begat Nimrod: he began to be a mighty one in the earth. 1 Chronicles 1:10 Cush begot Nimrod; he began to be a mighty one on the earth.

THE TWO BABYLONS BY ALEXANDER HISLOP

Kronos was the first king of Babylon, or Nimrod; consequently, the first centaur was the same.

Now, the way in which the centaur was represented on the Babylonian coins...

and in the Zodiac... is very striking: the centaur was the same as the sign Sagittarius, or "The Archer."

If the founder of Babylon's glory was "The Mighty Hunter," whose name, even in the days of Moses, was a Proverb...

Genesis 10:9 He was a mighty hunter before Yahweh: wherefore it is said, Even as Nimrod, the mighty hunter before Yahweh.

When we find the "Archer" with his bow as a symbol of the Supreme Babylonian Divinity...NIMROD!

And the "Archer" among the signs of the Zodiac that originated in Babylon, I think we may safely conclude that this Man-horse or Horse-man archer primarily referred to him {Nimrod}...

And was intended to perpetuate the memory at once of his fame as a huntsman and his skill as a horse breaker.

<u>Analytical Hebrew and Chaldee Lexicon, by Benjamin Davidson, Samuel Baggster and Sons, London, England, page 651</u>: Copyright 1871

The word "HUNTER" was translated from the original Hebrew word "TZUD," which has the meaning of hunter of men, to ensnare to beguile.

Nimrod's birthday was December 25, and how they produced the birth of the Christian sun deity Jesus. December 25 is the rebirth of all sun deities. Jesus Christ, Lord, God, Sacred, Amen, Adonai, and Angel are a few sun deity names that were put into the Word of Yahweh to propagandize that it was done by Constantine.

Yahweh's name was in the scriptures over 6000 times. Yet, anywhere a pagan deity name is spoken of, they got it right every time.

There were no kingdoms back then, only cities, and he WENT FORTH CONQUERING these cities and lands until he built the first kingdom on Earth. Nimrod was the king of the first kingdom on Earth, which was the beginning of the Babylonian Empire. This is why Nimrod represents the Babylonian Empire in verse 2 of Revelation Chapter 6.

As Genesis 10:8 states: "He began to be <u>a mighty one on the earth.</u>"

He defied Yahweh by building the "Tower of Babel," so Yahweh confounded the languages of the people and scattered them abroad.

Genesis 11:8-9

8 So Yahweh scattered them abroad from thence upon the face of all the earth: and they left off to build the city.

9 Therefore is the name of it called Babel; because Yahweh did there confound the language of all the earth: and from thence did Yahweh scatter them abroad upon the face of all the earth.

At the time of Constantine, the Roman Empire engulfed all of humanity in the known world. From the Tower of Babel to the era of Constantine's rule, people with new languages settled and moved to different lands due to wars or persecutions throughout history. This is how the United States was founded; today, its citizens speak over 400 languages, reflecting many diverse cultures.

This is how many pagan cultures were made. This is also the reason why there are so many sun deity names from all these diverse cultures, which worshiped Nimrod as the sun in all these different names.

Tower of Bable

Genesis 11: 1-9

1. And the whole earth was of one language and of one speech.
2. And it came to pass, as they journeyed from the East, that they found a plain in the land of Shinar; and they dwelt there.
3. And they said one to another, Go to, let us make brick, and burn them thoroughly. And they had brick for stone and tar for mortar.
4. And they said, Go to, let us build us a city and a tower, whose top may reach unto heaven; and let us make us a name, lest we be scattered abroad upon the face of the whole earth.
5. And YAHWEH CAME DOWN TO SEE the city and the tower, which the children of men built.
6. And Yahweh said, Behold, the people is one, and they have all one language; and this they begin to do: and now nothing will be restrained from them, which they have imagined to do.
7. Go to, LET US GO DOWN, and there confound their language, that they may not understand one another's speech.
8. So Yahweh scattered them abroad from thence upon the face of all the earth, and they left off to build the city.
9. Therefore is the name of it called Babel; because Yahweh did there confound the language of all the earth: and from thence did Yahweh scatter them abroad upon the face of all the earth.

According to The People's Bible Encyclopedia page 791, copyright 1924:

NIMROD is the name of a person mentioned in the Old (Covenant) as the son of Cush (Genesis 10:8 and 1 Chronicles 1:10). He was celebrated as a great hunter. To him is ascribed the foundation of the great Babylonian Empire and the building of the cities, which were afterward combined together under the general name of Nineveh. He, therefore, becomes also the founder of Assyria, and this country is therefore called by the prophet Micah (5:6) the land of Assyria.

So, *Nimrod is the rider on the WHITE HORSE; he brought false paganism into existence, and he was the first FALSE MESSIAH. Christianity will be the last-day religion of this Mystery Babylon religious system. Nimrod was the first Pontifex Maximus and the Pope who holds the title of Pontifex Maximus, and why he is called Pope is traced back to Nimrod and the same Babylonian Religious Government System that is being pushed today.*

Constantine was the last Emperor of the Roman Empire, and he started pagan Christianity. He changed the Roman Empire government from secular over religious to religious over secular government and became the first Pontifex Maximus over this Christianity and the Papacy government system that took the place of the emperors and secular over religious government.

Constantine was the one who covered up the truth of Yahweh and made it a lie after all the elect were killed off during the 11 Roman Emperor Persecutions. History of the cover-up of what Constantine had done teaches that there were only 10 Persecutions. This Babylonian religious system is what Yahweh will destroy at His coming, and it all started with Nimrod, and Constantine helped to carry it forward to the end times and its destruction by Yahweh Messiah.

NIMROD'S KINGDOM, or HIS CROWN, was GIVEN TO HIM. He had the first kingdom on this Earth.

The BOW represents a conqueror, a great hunter, and the HUNTER of the SOULS OF MEN with his false worship or paganism. When reading the scriptures where the word Gentile is used, you can exchange it for pagan or heathen.

Pontifex Maximus, that title was handed down through the empires, and today, the Pope holds that title. The throne of this Babylonian Religious System will end up in Zion since the Pope has that title now and why he is called Pope - the last one will move to Zion a few years before Yahweh returns. Christianity will become the last-day Mystery Babylonian religion when it becomes the global religion under the Papacy.

Nimrod was the first king, the first false messiah, and the first Pontifex Maximus. He was the first person after the flood that Satan influenced to rebel and lead others against Yahweh. Nimrod and his wife, Semiramis, were worshipped as deities, and from here is where this mother and son worship had started.

The Pope is traced back to Nimrod, not Peter. The reason the Popes seek to be worshiped as deities is rooted in the belief system that the last Pope, whom I believe will be Nimrod himself, will rule the world from Zion.

The two-horned MITRE worn by the Pope when he sits on the high altar in Rome and receives adoration from the Cardinals is the same Mitre worn by the priests of Dagon, the fish-deity of the Philistines and Babylonians.

- The Two Babylons by Alexander Hislop; p. 215, copyright 1903

The Mystery religion of ancient Babylon / Assyria was noted for the priestly class of Dagon in much the same way that the "Mystery" religion of Rome has copied it.

...there is strong evidence that Dagon was Nimrod.... All scholars agree that the name and worship of Dagon were imported from Babylonia.

The Religious "Mitre" Hat From Babylon | **The Priest of Ancient "Dagon" Fish Worship**

The Two Babylons, Hislop, p. 215, copyright 1903

"In their veneration and worship of Dagon, the high priest of paganism would put on a garment that had been created from a huge fish! The head of the fish formed a Mitre above that of the old man, while its scaly, fan-like tail fell as a cloak behind, leaving the human limbs and feet exposed."

Definition of "Ichthyic": "of, pertaining to, or characteristic of fishes; the fish world in all its orders."- Oxford English Dictionary (C. E.)

ICHTHYS, GREEK FOR FISH
PHILISTINE FISH-GOD DAGON

We know that Babylon is the origin of false worship and religion. Christianity absorbed all pagan religions with the Pontifex Maximus (Pope) over it.

Revelation 17:5 And upon her forehead (Zion) was a name written, Mystery, Babylon the Great, The Mother of Harlots and Abominations of The Earth.

CHAPTER 2
PRELUDE TO CONSTANTINE

BEFORE THE PERSECUTIONS STARTED, THIS IS WHAT THE ELECT WERE TOLD TO DO.

Luke 24: 47- 49

47 And that repentance and remission of transgressions should be taught in His name to all nations, HIS NAME IS YAHWEH, THEY ARE NOT TEACHING HIS NAME TODAY, IT IS ONLY ANTI-MESSIAH NAMES THEY ALL USE AND TEACH. And if they use Yahweh's name it is not used for the Messiah's name.

48 And you are witnesses of these things.

49 And behold, I send the promise of my Father upon you: but tarry ye in the city of Zion, until ye be endued with power from on high.

Acts 1: 4, 5, 8

4 And, being assembled together with them, commanded them that they should not depart from Zion, but wait for the promise of the Father, which, saith he, ye have heard of me.

5 For John truly baptized with water; but ye shall be baptized with the Spirit not many days hence.

8 But ye shall receive power, after that the Spirit is come upon you: and ye shall be witnesses unto me both in Zion, and in all Judea, and in Samaria, and unto the uttermost part of the earth.

Matt. 28:19 Go ye therefore, and teach all nations, baptizing them in the name of the Father, and of the Son, and of the Spirit (Yahweh):

YES, THE NAME THEY BAPTIZED IN WAS YAHWEH AND NO OTHER.

Mark 16: 15-20

[15] And he said unto them, Go ye into all the world, and teach the word to every creature.

[16] He that believes and is baptized shall be saved; but he that believes not shall be condemned.

[17] And these signs shall follow them that believe; In my name shall they cast out devils; they shall speak with new tongues;

[18] They shall take up serpents; and if they drink any deadly thing, it shall not hurt them; they shall lay hands on the sick and they shall recover.

(Notice: It does not say MIGHT but SHALL.)

[19] So then, after Immanuel had spoken unto them, he was received up into heaven, and sat on the right hand of Yahweh.

(Remember, scriptures speak of only one throne, not two.)

[20] And they went forth, and "TAUGHT" everywhere, Yahweh working with them, and confirming the word with signs following.

In the following verse, Paul says that the Word was "taught" to every creature under heaven. BACK THEN!

Colossians 1:23 If ye continue in the faith grounded and settled and be not moved away from the hope of the word, which ye have heard, and which was "taught" to every creature which is under the heaven; whereof I Paul am made a teacher. *(Notice Paul did not make himself a teacher, but he says, "He was made a teacher." This could only have come from Yahweh.)*

Mark 16:16 *He that believeth and is baptized shall be saved; but he that believeth not shall be damned.*

You see, the whole world back then had a choice to BELIEVE or NOT TO BELIEVE. OUR ANCESTORS WERE THE ONES WHO DID NOT BELIEVE, AND WE INHERITED THEIR LIES. THE FALLING AWAY TOOK PLACE BACK THEN.

CONSTANTINE:

Constantine—born February 27, after 280 C.E.—died May 22, 337

Revelation 12:9,12

9 And the great dragon was cast out, that old serpent, called the Devil, and Satan, which DECEIVES THE WHOLE WORLD: he was cast out into the earth, and his messengers were cast out with him. 12 Therefore rejoice, ye heavens, and ye that dwell in them. Woe to the inhabiters of the earth and of the sea! for the devil is come down unto you, having great wrath, because he knoweth that he hath but a short time.

Satan was laying the foundation for every system of falsehood and error the world has ever known.

Romans 1:25 They took the truth of Yahweh and turned it into a lie and "worshiped and served created things rather than the Creator."

This system of paganism, while professing to be the truth, is Satan worship. It professes and claims to be the truth of Yahweh, but it is Satan's masterpiece, the *"mystery of iniquity."*

John 4:20-21

²⁰ Our fathers worshiped in this mountain; and ye say, that in Zion is the place where men ought to worship.

²¹ Immanuel saith unto her, Woman, believe me, THE HOUR COMETH, WHEN YE SHALL NEITHER IN THIS MOUNTAIN, NOR YET AT ZION, WORSHIP THE FATHER.

They worshiped the Father all the way up to Constantine, who killed off the last of Yahweh Messiah's elect. Subsequently, Yahweh gave man over to their own reprobate minds, allowing them to believe a lie.

There is no other time in human history when Satan could deceive the entire world, except from the time of Constantine—after he killed off the last of Yahweh's elect—up to the coming 7-Year Peace Plan, when salvation is offered again.

Revelation 6:8 *And I looked and behold a pale horse: and his name that sat on him was Death, and the grave followed with him (emperors). And power was given unto them (Emperors) over the fourth part of the earth (Roman Empire engulfed the whole of humanity), to kill with sword, and with hunger, and with death, and with the beasts of the earth.*

Revelation 13:2 *And the beast which I saw was like unto a leopard, and his feet were as the feet of a bear, and his mouth as the mouth of a lion: and the dragon gave him his power, and his seat, and great authority.*

BEFORE THE PERSECUTIONS STARTED THIS IS WHAT THE ELECT WERE TOLD TO DO.

Luke 24:47- 49

47 "And that repentance and remission of transgressions should be taught in His name to all nations." HIS NAME IS YAHWEH, THEY ARE NOT TEACHING HIS NAME TODAY, IT IS ONLY ANTI - MESSIAH NAMES THEY ALL USE AND TEACH. And if they use Yahweh's name it is not used for the Messiah's name.

48 And you are witnesses of these things.

49 And behold, I send the promise of my Father upon you: but tarry ye in the city of Zion, until ye be endued with power from on high.

Acts 1:4,5,8 CORRECTED

4 And, being assembled together with them, commanded them that they should not depart from Zion, but wait for the promise of the Father, which, saith he, ye have heard of me.

5 For John truly baptized with water; but ye shall be baptized with the Spirit not many days hence.

8 But ye shall receive power, after that the Spirit is come upon you: and ye shall be witnesses unto me both in Zion, and in all Judea, and in Samaria, and unto the uttermost part of the earth

Matt. 28:19 Go ye therefore, and teach all nations, baptizing them in the name of the Father, and of the Son, and of the Spirit (Yahweh):

THE HOUSE OF YAHWEH WAS DESTROYED IN 70 C.E.

2 Chronicles 29:20-26

^{20} Then Hezekiah the king rose early, and gathered the rulers of the city, and went up to the HOUSE OF YAHWEH.

^{21} And they brought seven bullocks, and seven rams, and seven lambs, and seven he goats, for a transgression offering for the kingdom, and for the place of refuge, and for Judah. And he commanded the priests the sons of Aaron to offer them on the altar of Yahweh.

^{22} So they killed the bullocks, and the priests received the blood, and sprinkled it on the altar: likewise, when they had killed the rams, they sprinkled the blood upon the altar: they killed also the lambs, and they sprinkled the blood upon the altar.

^{23} And they brought forth the he goats for the sin offering before the king and the congregation; and they laid their hands upon them: 24 And the priests killed them, and they made reconciliation with their blood upon the altar, to make an atonement for all Judaea: for the king commanded that the burnt offering and the transgression offering should be made for all Israel.

^{25} And he set the Levites in the HOUSE OF YAHWEH with cymbals, with psalteries, and with harps, according to the commandment of David, and of Gad the king's seer, and Nathan the prophet: for so was the commandment of Yahweh by his prophets.

^{26} And the Levites stood with the instruments of David, and the priests with the trumpets.

THE ABOVE VERSES pretty much represents what I am speaking of........ They mention the House of Yahweh which was destroyed for the last time in 70 A.D. and there will not be another built until the Millennial Kingdom by Yahweh Himself. Jews never used Synagogues or Temples, only the pagans did in their worship, Jews used the House of Yahweh. The Messiah became the High Priest after the order of Melchizedek priesthood. So, without the House of Yahweh, there was no need for the Levite priesthood to do the animal offerings and collecting the tithes and other duties.. Tithes could only be collected by the Levites and Yahweh did away with tithing and gave man a better way in the New Covenant with giving the Messiah for the transgressions of man, so animal offerings were done away with too. Once again, no need for the Levites, UNTIL THE MILLENNIAL KINGDOM,, why? Because Yahweh will raise all those that had died and never heard the truth with the opportunity for salvation all the way up to the Papacy's 7 Year Peace Plan that will end WW3, back to Constantine when this world became completely Satan's. At the time of the Peace Plan salvation will be available again to all the living as the truth is taught again through Moses and Eliyah. The reason the Levites will start transgression animal offerings is because the people who are raised and taught the truth by Yahweh himself will not have any forgiveness of transgressions, this will bring back the need for animal offerings done by the Levites. These people are the ones that Satan will try to deceive at the end of the Millennium, when he is raised again. They have a choice to serve Yahweh or Satan, if Yahweh, he will fill those with his Spirit, if Satan he will burn them up at the White throne judgement. Their choice!

Jews celebrated the festival of Sukkot on the Mount of Olives. They made pilgrimages to the Mount of Olives because it was 80 meters (262 and about half a foot) higher than the House of Yahweh / Mount Moriah and offered a panoramic view of Mount Moriah since no one really knew where the House of Yahweh sat, the location has been found, which was destroyed in 70 C.E.

There is only one mount near Zion, which looks like a skull of a head. And this mount is only 330 meters higher than where the House of Yahweh entrance once supposedly stood, the Mount of Olives. The Mount of Olives is where the death took place.

Immanuel was killed on the Mount of Olives, so there must have been plenty of olive trees on the Mount of Olives to be named that. Josephus relates that Titus cut down all the trees in the besiege of Zion in 70 C.E.

Luke 21:37 *And in the day time he was teaching in the House of Yahweh; and at night he went out, and abode in the mount that is called the Mount of Olives.*

John 19:17 *And he bearing his yoke went forth into a place called the place of a skull, which is called in the Hebrew Golgotha:*

Revelation 1:15 *His feet were like fine brass, as if refined in a furnace, and His voice as the sound of many waters;*

The verses mentioned above and below are speaking of the feet of his Mothership where his throne is, not his feet on his body. The spacecraft will move the mountain. The Mothership will be humongous.

Zechariah 14:4 *And his feet shall stand in that day upon the Mount of Olives, which is before Zion on the East, and the Mount of Olives shall cleave in the midst thereof toward the East and toward the West, and there shall be a very great valley; and half of the mountain shall remove toward the North, and half of it toward the South.*

This is where Yahweh's Mothership will land and sit on the Mount of Olives.

Acts 1:11-12

[11] Which also said, Ye men of Galilee, why stand ye gazing up into heaven: This same Yahweh, which is taken up from you into heaven, shall so come in like manner as ye have seen him go into heaven.

In a spacecraft.

The Romans rebuilt Zion in 135 C.E. The walls were reconstructed upon the foundations of the walls built during the time of the Second House of Yahweh and the later Roman expansion. The present walls around the Old City were built from 1537 to 1541 by Sultan Suleiman the Magnificent following the Ottoman conquest of Judah. At that time, most of the ancient walls had been reduced to rubble. Suleiman ordered Zion to be fortified to protect its people against marauding Bedouins. For the most part, the modern gates of the city are not closely related to the walls and gates that existed in Roman times or earlier. There is some debate about the correct location of some of the ancient gates and walls. However, visitors to the recently restored Jewish Quarter in the Old City can see an uncovered section of the wall built by Nehemiah at the time of the return from the Babylonian exile. This gate, the oldest of all the city gates, was the only one not rebuilt by Suleiman the Magnificent in C.E. 1539-42. Monolithic stones in the wall just above the ground have been identified as 5th Century B.C.E masonry from the time of Nehemiah (Biblical Archaeological Review [BAR], Mar/Apr 1992, p40).

The Zion we see today is not the Zion that the Messiah walked. Moreover, today's Judaea is a Papacy deceit called Israel. Yahweh will bring back all 12 tribes during the 7-Year Peace Plan; the last 3 1/2 years are the Tribulation years. It will be the 144,000 from the 12 tribes who are given salvation and are the last ones to receive it right before Yahweh Messiah's return when all the world's armies will go against Zion. It will be the 144,000 mentioned in Revelation Chapter 7 who will call Yahweh back.

CHAPTER 3
CONSTANTINE IS THE LITTLE HORN OF DANIEL 7

FOURTH SEAL - ROMAN EMPIRE - PALE HORSE

Revelation 6:8:

Seals

Fourth Seal / Pale Horse = Roman Empire (63 BCE - WE ARE STILL LIVING IN THE ERA OF THE ROMAN EMPIRE TODAY, THE POPES TOOK THE PLACE OF THE EMPERORS.

Daniel 2:33 & 40:

- The Image of a Man
- Legs of Iron = Roman Empire

Daniel 7:7:

- The 4 Beasts
- 4th Beast
- Beast with Iron Teeth = Roman Empire

Revelation 13:2

Beast - PAPACY BEAST - 1 And I stood upon the sand of the sea, and saw a beast rise up out of the sea, having seven heads and ten horns, and upon his horns ten crowns, and upon his heads the name of blasphemy.

And the beast (PAPACY) which I saw was like unto a leopard (GRECIAN EMPIRE), and his feet were as the feet of a bear (MEDIO PERSIAN EMPIRE), and his mouth as the mouth of a lion (BABYLONIAN EMPIRE): and the dragon (SATAN) gave him his power, and his seat, and great authority.

You must remember that the POPES TOOK THE PLACE OF THE EMPERORS THAT ALSO HELD THE TITLE OF PONTIFEX MAXIMUS.

LUKE 4:5-7

5 And the devil, taking him up on a high mountain, shewed unto him all the kingdoms of the world in a moment of time.

6 And the devil said unto him, All this power will I give thee, and the glory of them: for that is delivered unto me; and to whomsoever I will I give it.

SO WHO DID SATAN GIVE IT TO? HE GAVE IT TO THE EMPERORS AND CONSTANTINE WAS THE FIRST PONTIFEX MAXIMUS THAT NOT ONLY STARTED THE PAPACY BUT WAS ALSO

THE FIRST POPE OVER HIS PAGAN CHRISTIANITY. WE ARE STILL LIVING IN THE ERA OF THE ROMAN EMPIRE WHICH NEVER FELL BUT WAS CHANGED FROM AN EMPEROR SECULAR GOVERNMENT TO A PAPACY RELIGIOUS GOVERNMENT..

7 If thou therefore wilt worship me, all shall be thine.

8 And Immanuel answered and said unto him, Get thee behind me, Satan: for it is written, Thou shalt worship Yahweh thy Mighty One, and him only shalt thou serve.

Revelation 6:8 And I looked, and behold a pale horse: and his name that sat on him was Death, and the grave followed with him (EMPEROR). And power was given unto them (Emperors) over the fourth part of the earth, to kill with sword, and with hunger, and with death, and with the beasts of the earth.

THE PALE HORSE REPRESENTS: DEATH /EMPEROR

The Pale Horse rider is Death / Emperor. (THEM) The Emperors of Rome. Today that is the Pope who sits under Saint Peter's Dome. The Roman Empire killed Yahweh's people in many a way. The believers all died for their savior, Messiah Yahweh.

Daniel 7:20-21 - THE LITTLE HORN IS Constantine WHO WAS THE FIRST POPE OVER CHRISTIANITY AND HE STARTED THE PAPACY.

20 And of the ten horns that were in his head, and of the other which came up, and before whom three fell; even of that horn that had eyes, and a mouth that spake very great things, whose look was more stout than his fellows.

21 I beheld, and the same horn/ Constantine made war with the saints / ELECT, and prevailed against them;

Revelation 12:11

11 And they overcame him by the blood of the Lamb, and by the word of their testimony; and they loved not their lives unto the death.

The last of the Spirit filled Elect were all killed off by Constantine with his 11th Roman Emperor Persecution and Yahweh took his Spirit of salvation away and why there is no salvation available since that time and even up today.

Daniel 8:23-25

23 And in the latter time of their kingdom, when the transgressors are come to the full, a king of fierce countenance, and understanding dark sentences, shall stand up.

24 And his power shall be mighty, but not by his own power: and he shall destroy wonderfully, and shall prosper, and practice, and shall destroy the mighty and the RIGHTEOUS people.

25 And through his policy also he shall cause craft to prosper in his hand; and he shall magnify himself in his heart, and by peace shall destroy many: he shall also stand up against the King of Kings; but he shall be broken without hand.

Revelation 2:10-12

10 Fear none of those things which thou shalt suffer: behold, Satan shall cast some of you into prison, that ye may be tried; and ye shall have TRIBULATION ten days: be thou faithful unto death, and I will give thee a crown of life.

11 He that hath an ear, let him hear what the Spirit saith unto the assemblies; He that overcometh shall not be hurt of the second death.

Revelation 12:11 And they overcame him by the blood of the Lamb, and by the word of their testimony; and they loved not their lives unto the death.

2 Thessalonians 2:8-12

[8] And then shall that Wicked be revealed, whom Yahweh shall consume with the spirit of his mouth, and shall destroy with the brightness of his coming:

[9] Even him, whose coming is after the working of Satan with all power and signs and lying wonders,

[10] And with all deceivableness of unrighteousness in them that perish; because they received not the love of the truth, that they might be saved.

[11] And for this cause Yahweh shall send them strong delusion, that they should believe a lie:

[12] That they all might be damned who believed not the truth, but had pleasure in unrighteousness.

Story of Nations - 1956, page 152:

The Emperor Nero murdered thousands of Christians/ (the Elect) whom he falsely accused of setting fire to the city. Many (of the) devout Christians/ (Elect) were thrown to hungry wild beasts in the arenas, to provide the Romans entertainment, as well as to discourage the spread of (the) Christianity / (FAITH IN YAHWEH MESSIAH).

Exploring The Old World - 1965, page 131:

TO STAMP OUT Christianity / (the FAITH in Yahweh Messiah), Christians / (the Elect) were thrown to lions, crucified, burned alive, or killed by gladiators.

Revelation 6:8 And I looked, and behold a pale horse: and his name that sat on him was Death, and the grave followed with him (EMPEROR). And power was given unto them (Emperors) over the fourth part of the earth, to kill with sword, and with hunger, and with death, and with the beasts of the earth.

NOTICE: That crucifixion is not mentioned in the above verse, nor being burned alive, yet history has added both because the Papacy changed history to support their lies.

And this was not the religion of Christianity, that they wanted to stamp out. This was the very reason why Christianity was created, so that it could absorb all other religions.

One thing that is missing about Nero is that he couldn't possibly have persecuted Christians, since Christianity did not exist until the 4th century. THERE WAS A PAGAN RELIGION BY THE SAME NAME, BUT THEY WERE NOT KILLED DURING THE PERSECUTIONS.

Matthew 24:34

Verily I say unto you, This generation shall not pass, till all these things be fulfilled.

There were ten periods of persecutions from Emperor Nero being the first in 64 C.E., to Emperor Diocletian in 303 C.E. varying in length. These are the 4th Seal

History will teach you that there were only Ten Roman Persecutions when there was Eleven.

Emperor

Emperor/Date (A.D.)

1. Nero 54-68

2. Domitian 81-96

3. Trajan 98-117

4. Marcus Aurelius 161-180

5. Septimius Severus 193-211

6. Maximinus the Thracian 235-238

7. Decius Trajan 249-251

8. Valerian 253-260

9. Lucius Aurelian 270-275

10. Diocletian 284-305

11. Constantine ruled from 306 -337

Roman Empire was changed to a religious government under Constantine.

Diocletian died in 305 and Constantine took over in 306 so Constantine continued Diocletian's Persecution as his own.

The last (the 11th) persecution (of Constantine's) ended in 313.

311 CE – The Edict of Toleration by Galerius was issued in 311 by the Roman Tetrarchy of Galerius, Constantine and Licinius,

officially ending the Diocletian persecution of Christianity; this is not true Constantine was covering up his own Persecution.

Daniel 7:21 I beheld, and the same horn made war with the Elect, and prevailed against them;

The Little Horn of Daniel is Constantine and he killed off the last of Yahweh's Elect with the 11th Roman Emperor Persecution. See how they covered up what Constantine did by acting like Constantine was ending Diocletian Persecution and not his own.?

313 – Roman Emperors Constantine I and Licinius issued the Edict of Milan that legalized Christianity across the whole Empire.

The Little Horn of Daniel is Constantine and he killed off the last of Yahweh's Elect.

Edict of Milan, proclamation that permanently established religious toleration for Christianity within the Roman Empire. It was the outcome of a political agreement concluded in Mediolanum (modern Milan) between the Roman emperors Constantine I and Licinius in February 313. WHO issued the Edict of Toleration?

CONSTANTINE KILLED OFF THE LAST OF YAHWEH'S ELECT WITH THE 11TH PERSECUTION. THE BOOKS OF DANIEL AND REVELATION ARE CONNECTED WITH THE LITTLE HORN OF CHAPTER 7 AND THE 4TH SEAL OF REVELATION CHAPTER 6.

Back to Daniel 7:21

21 I beheld, and the same horn made war with the elect, and prevailed against them;

EMPEROR WHO BECAME POPE CONSTANTINE KILLED OFF THE LAST OF YAHWEH'S ELECT BACK THEN.

After Nero came the persecutions from Emperor Domitian then Emperor Decius in 250 C.E., after him came Emperor Valerian in 257 to 258 C.E., and finally the last of the 10 and worst under Emperor Diocletian who began his rule in 284 C.E., and his persecutions started in 303 C.E. and his rule ended in 305 C.E., while Maximian was Emperor of the West. Constantine finished them off with the 11th Roman Emperor Persecution.

All books, records, and writings were confiscated and burned, like in other persecutions. Every person including children suspected of being of the faith in Yahweh were killed without recourse to laws or by any other means. Horsemen rode across the empire with a public proclamation of extermination.

Constantine ruled from 306 to 337 C.E., in 312 C.E., he was proclaimed Emperor by the Senate, he made Christianity in 313 (Edict of Milan), the official state religion of the Roman Empire.

THE ROMAN EMPIRE (4TH SEAL - PALE HORSE)

"And I looked, and behold a pale horse: and his name that sat on him was Death, and the grave followed with him. And power was given unto THEM {EMPERORS} over the fourth part of the earth, to kill with sword, and with hunger, and with death, and with the beasts of the earth."

"And they overcame him {Satan} by the blood of the Lamb, and by the word of their testimony; for they loved not their lives even unto their death." This was done by the ten Roman persecutions until the last one took their last breath. They all were laid to rest and each and every one was surely blessed.

Daniel 7:7-8

7 After this I saw in the night visions, and behold a fourth beast, dreadful and terrible, and strong exceedingly; and it had great iron teeth: it devoured and brake in pieces and stamped the residue with the feet of it: and it was diverse from all the beasts that were before it; and it had ten horns.

THIS IS THE ROMAN EMPIRE.

10 Horns are the Roman emperors that persecuted and killed the Elect of Yahweh Messiah. CONSTANTINE WAS THE ELEVENTH—the Little Horn that rose out of the 10 horns.

THE 11 ROMAN EMPERORS WHO INITIATED AND CONCLUDED THE PERSECUTIONS THAT WOULD END UP KILLING OFF ALL YAHWEH MESSIAH'S ELECT. History only acknowledges 10 persecutions, even though there were eleven, and Constantine instigated the eleventh and final persecution that killed the last of Yahweh's elect. He ended up being different from the first 10 emperors.

1. Nero's Persecution (64-68)
2. Domitian's Persecution (90–96)
3. Trajan's Persecution (98–117)
4. Hadrian's Persecution (117–138)
5. Marcus Aurelius's Persecution (161–180)
6. Septimius Severus' Persecution (202–211)
7. Maximinus' Persecution (235–236)
8. Decius' Persecution (249–251)

9.   Valerian's Persecution (257–260)
10.   Diocletian's Persecution (284-305)
11.   Constantine's Persecution (306-311)

They tried to portray Constantine's persecution as a continuation of Diocletian's persecution. However, Constantine's was a distinct one and had his own separate and unique characteristics.

⁸ I considered the horns, and behold, <u>there came up among them another little horn, before whom there were three of the first horns plucked up by the roots</u>: and behold, in this horn were eyes like the eyes of man, and a mouth speaking great things.

EMPEROR DIOCLETIAN SPLIT THE EMPIRE INTO 2, CREATING A RULE OF 4.

At the time of Constantine's rise to power, the West was governed by Constantine and Maxentius, while the East had Maximus (original name Daia) and Licinius.

1. In 312 C.E., Constantine defeated Maxentius in the Battle of the Milvian Bridge near Rome, securing his control over the Western Roman Empire.
2. Licinius defeated Maximinus, who then committed suicide.
3. In 324 C.E., he defeated Licinius, the Eastern Roman emperor, in the Battle of Chrysocolla, thus becoming the sole ruler of the Roman Empire.
4. Constantine fought his rivals for the throne and finally established himself as the sole ruler in 324 CE.

THESE ARE THE 3 FIRST HORNS THAT WERE PLUCKED UP BEFORE CONSTANTINE, THE LITTLE HORN, WOULD SHOW UP AMONG THE 10 HORNS—THE PERSECUTING POWERS (PLUCKED UP BY THE ROOTS, MEANS KILLED).

1. MAXENTIUS

2. MAXIMINUS

3. LUCINIUS

Constantine became the fourth one.

These 3 Horns had to be removed so Constantine could become the sole ruler of the Roman Empire.

THE 10 HORNS ARE THE ROMAN EMPERORS THAT PERSECUTED AND KILLED YAHWEH'S ELECT. CONSTANTINE CAME UP OUT OF THESE, THE LITTLE HORN.

AT THE TIME OF CONSTANTINE, WHEN HE STARTED TO COME INTO POWER, THE WEST HAD CONSTANTINE AND MAXENTIUS; THE EAST HAD MAXIMINUS DAIA AND LICINIUS.

THE LITTLE HORN IS CONSTANTINE:

MAXENTIUS WAS DEFEATED IN 312 BY CONSTANTINE AT MELVINA BRIDGE, WHERE CONSTANTINE SUPPOSEDLY SAW A CROSS IN THE SKY, SAYING, "IN THIS SIGN CONQUER." THE CROSS WILL BE THE MARK OF THE BEAST, A SUN SYMBOL SINCE CONSTANTINE WAS A SUN WORSHIPER. It became the symbol for Christianity, and now you can see how and why the cross ended up being the Mark of the Beast when the Papacy will make Christianity the world religion during the Tribulation Period.

LICINIUS DEFEATED MAXIMINUS, WHO ENDED UP KILLING HIMSELF, AND CONSTANTINE 324 DEFEATED LICINIUS AND BECAME THE SOLE RULER OF THE ROMAN EMPIRE.

CONSTANTINE KILLED OFF THE LAST OF YAHWEH'S ELECT WITH THE 11TH EMPEROR PERSECUTION.

CONSTANTINE CHANGED THE ROMAN EMPIRE'S GOVERNMENT FROM SECULAR TO RELIGIOUS AND BECAME THE FIRST POPE OR

PONTIFEX MAXIMUS OVER THE CHRISTIAN RELIGION, WHICH HE HAD STARTED TO ABSORB ALL PAGAN RELIGIONS. IT WAS CONSTANTINE WHO STARTED THE BABYLONIAN RELIGIOUS GOVERNMENT SYSTEM, THE PAPACY.

9 I beheld till the thrones were cast down, and the Ancient of days did sit, whose garment was white as snow, and the hair of his head like the pure wool: his throne was like the fiery flame, and his wheels as burning fire.

THIS PAPACY SYSTEM WITH THE POPE WAS BEHELD THROUGHOUT HISTORY TO THE END-TIME DESTRUCTION OF IT.

Constantine created Satanic Christianity to send people to the Lake of Fire, not to save them from it. He did so to absorb all pagan religions. Constantine WAS THE BEGINNING LITTLE HORN; THE LAST POPE WILL BE THE ONE GIVEN TO THE BURNING FLAME OR LAKE OF FIRE AT YAHWEH'S RETURN. ALSO, THE MUSLIMS WILL ACCEPT HIM AS THE MAHDI THAT THEY ARE WAITING FOR.

THE DECEITFUL TREE

There was a tree that started growing from its unaltered roots. As it grew, it started to become a majestic oak, but something happened. As the branches started to grow from the trunk, new branches were grafted to take their place. Branches from an apple, evergreen, maple, fig, walnut tree, and so on. As the tree grew, new branches were grafted in. As these branches took hold, the tree started growing its own smaller branches from these. Finally, when it was fully grown it looked like a tree that no one had ever seen before. The tree appealed to all humanity. All the grafting on this tree concealed the original kind of tree it was. The name that was picked for this new looking tree, was Christianity.

By Gary W. Stanfield

[10] A fiery stream issued and came forth from before him: thousand thousands ministered unto him, and ten thousand times ten thousand stood before him: the judgment was set, and the books were opened.

THIS PAPACY GOVERNMENT SYSTEM IS WHAT YAHWEH WILL DESTROY AT HIS COMING.

[11] I beheld then because of the voice of the great words which the horn spake: I beheld even till the beast was slain, and his body destroyed, and given to the burning flame.

CHAPTER 4
THE GREAT FALLING AWAY

Acts 20:28-31

28 Take heed therefore unto yourselves, and to all the flock, over the which the Spirit hath made you overseers, to feed the assembly of Yahweh, which He hath purchased with His own blood.

29 For I know this, that after my departing shall grievous wolves enter in among you, not sparing the flock.

30 Also of your own selves shall men arise, speaking perverse things, to draw away disciples after them.

31 Therefore watch, and remember, that by the space of three years I ceased not to warn every one night and day with tears.

Romans 1:28

And even as they did not like to retain Yahweh in their knowledge, Yahweh gave them over to a reprobate mind, to do those things which are not convenient;

2 Thessalonians 2:11

10 And with all deceivableness of unrighteousness in them that perish; because they received not the love of the truth, that they might be saved.

11 For this reason Yahweh sends them a powerful delusion, so that they will believe the lie.

1 John 2: 22, 23

[22] Who is a liar but he that denieth that Yahweh is the Messiah? He is Anti-Messiah, that denieth the Father and the Son.

[23] Whosoever denieth the Son, the same hath not the Father: he that acknowledgeth the Son hath the Father also.

Proverbs 30:4 Who hath ascended up into heaven, or descended? Who hath gathered the wind in his fists? Who hath bound the waters in a garment? Who hath established all the ends of the earth? What is his name, and what is his son's name, if thou canst tell? (THE NAME IS YAHWEH)

1 John 4:1-3

[1] Beloved, believe not every spirit, but try the spirits whether they are of Yahweh: because many false prophets are gone out into the world.

[2] Hereby know ye the Spirit of Yahweh: Every spirit that confesseth that Yahweh Messiah is come in the flesh is of Yahweh:

[3] And every spirit that confesseth not that Yahweh Messiah is come in the flesh is not of Yahweh: and this is that spirit of Anti-Messiah, whereof ye have heard that it should come; and even now already is it in the world.

1 John 2:18 Little children, it is the last time: and as ye have heard that the Anti-Messiah shall come, even now are there many Anti-Messiahs; whereby we know that it is the last time.

2 John 1:7 For many deceivers are entered into the world, who confess not that Yahweh Messiah is come in the flesh. This is the deceiver and the Anti-Messiah.

Acts 18:28 For he mightily convinced the Jews, and that publicly, showing by the scriptures that Yahweh was the Messiah.

NOTE: *The name of Jesus Christ, or any other name, Yahshua, Yeshua, are all anti-Messiah names and any other name people may try to use for salvation.*

The falling away happened during the 11 Roman Emperor persecutions. Christianity wants you to believe it did not happen back then, but it had already occurred; it is presented as a future event, but Yahweh will do a quick work with the coming 3 ½ Year Tribulation Period, the last one lasting 247 years.

Constantine ended the 4th Seal, and by doing that, he opened the 5th Seal, which is the rule of the Papacy. We are living at the very end of it as we watch the Papacy regaining its power for these end-times.

CHAPTER 5
CONSTANTINE FULFILLED PROPHECIES

THE FOLLOWING ARE THE THINGS THAT CONSTANTINE DID TO FULFILL PROPHECIES:

1. He became the Little Horn of Daniel 7.
2. Constantine started the Babylonian Religious Government System – religious over the secular government. This is what the two-horned lamb represents: an entity set on ruling the world, THE PAPACY, from Emperor Rome to Papal Rome. The Papacy is using Socialism to rule the world. The Jesuits started Marxism, Communism, Fascism, and Nazism, and all forms of Socialism. In the mid-1800s, they started Social Justice / Reform, which you hear so much about today. They are behind gun control, illegal aliens, abortion, and countries without borders. They are either buying hospitals and medical facilities or using other ways to control them. One day, they will say who will live and who will die. The Jesuits also played a crucial role in the modern education system. This is how they are controlling what is being taught in schools and colleges – brainwashing kids to fulfill their agendas. Educational institutions are the places where Anti-Semitism and many other agendas are taught to kids to further their agenda. They even get the kids to protest on their behalf. They are behind Black Lives Matter and all this LGBT Stuff. Another very alarming agenda that they are pushing is to get rid of parental rights and mess up the morality in the minds of the children.

3. Constantine closed the 4th Seal with the last Roman Emperor Persecution, resulting in the killing of the last of Yahweh's Elect.

4. Constantine opened the 5th Seal after he had killed the last of Yahweh's Elect at the end of the 4th Seal.

5. Constantine revealed what the Mark of the Beast/Papacy would be – the Cross. This happened when he said that he had seen a Cross in the sky with the words, "With this sign, conquer." A symbol of Christianity.

6. Constantine created Christianity, the religion that would become the end-time world religion under the Papacy and Pope.

THE DECEITFUL TREE

There was a tree that started growing from its unaltered roots. As it grew, it started to become a majestic oak, but something happened. As the branches started to grow from its trunk, new branches were grafted to take their place. Branches from an apple, evergreen, maple, fig, walnut tree, and so on. As the tree grew, new branches were grafted in. As these branches took hold, the tree started growing its own smaller branches from these. Finally, when it was fully grown, it looked like a tree that no one had ever seen before. The tree appealed to all mankind. All the grafting to this tree concealed the original kind of tree it was. The name that was picked for this new-looking tree was Christianity.

7. Constantine started this secular/religious government called the Papacy, which would rule the world before the coming of Yahweh Messiah.

8. Constantine was the first Pope of the religion known as Christianity.

Revelation 13:11 And I beheld another beast coming up out of the earth; and he had "two horns like a lamb," and he Spake as a dragon. Religious over secular government.

The two horns represent secular and religious governments each. This lamb-like person (Pope) comes in peaceably, but these governments are of Satan.

"The Papacy is but the ghost of the Roman Empire, sitting crowned upon the grave thereof."

On 21 June 325 C.E., Constantine convened the First Council of Nicaea, during which Christians professed the Nicene Creed. This event marks the inaugural ecclesiastical gathering in history and is now recognized as the Council of Nicaea. The meeting provided a peculiar insight into early clerical thinking, offering a clear depiction of the intellectual climate of the time. Christianity's inception can be traced back to this assembly, and the consequences of the decisions made are challenging to quantify.

Approximately four years before presiding over the Council, Constantine had been initiated into the religious order of Sol Invictus, one of the two thriving cults that regarded the Sun as the sole Supreme God (the other being Mithraism). Due to his Sun worship, he directed Eusebius to organize the first of three sessions on the summer solstice, 21 June 325 (Catholic Encyclopedia, New Edition, vol. i, p. 792), and the gathering took place "in a hall of Osius's palace" (Ecclesiastical History, Bishop Louis Dupin, Paris, 1986, vol. I, p. 598).

Pagan religions disappeared after Christianity became the State religion of the Roman Empire because Constantine did not allow any other religions; instead, Christianity absorbed them.

Why did Constantine's letter, issued at Nicaea, genuinely choose this Equinox date to celebrate the resurrection of the Christian Jesus? It is because the sun's activity during the spring Equinox is recognized in Constantine's pagan religion as the day when the death of winter is reversed. This day and each day thereafter are viewed as the "strengthening" of the sun, perceived as a resurrection of the Sun-God Sol Invictus from the death of winter (source: "Easter," Rev. George Lemon, English Etymology, 1783).

From his extensive research into Church councils, Dr. Watson concluded that "the clergy at the Council of Nicaea were all under the power of the devil, and the convention was composed of the lowest rabble and patronized the vilest abominations" (An Apology for Christianity, op. cit.). It was that infantile body of men who were responsible for the commencement of a new religion and the theological creation of Jesus Christ.

Constantine was the predominant figure in Nicaea, and he ultimately made the decision regarding a new deity for them. To involve British factions, he ruled that the name of the Druid deity, Hesus, should be combined with the Eastern Saviour-God, Krishna (Krishna is Sanskrit for Christ), resulting in Hesus Krishna becoming the official name of the new Roman God. A vote was conducted, and it was through a majority show of hands (161 votes to 157) that both divinities were merged into one God. Following the longstanding heathen custom, Constantine utilized the official gathering and the Roman apotheosis decree to legally deify two deities as one, doing so by democratic consent. A new God was proclaimed and "officially" ratified by Constantine (Acta Concilii Nicaeni, 1618).

Scriptures have been manipulated over the years by figures such as Constantine and Jerome, leading to doubts about their authenticity. The absence of original texts is a concern unless the Vatican possesses them, prompting scholars to engage in studies to uncover more truth from the scriptures.

Under Constantine and subsequent rulers, the Roman Empire spanned over one thousand years, encompassing 14, 25, or 40 generations, depending on the accepted duration of a generation—some suggest 70 years, others 40 years, and still others 25 years. This extended timeframe was utilized to perpetuate:

1. Mixed pagan religions, including Judaism to make Christianity.
2. Added pagan holidays like Christmas and Easter to influence pagans to come over to Christianity.
3. Collected all existing manuscripts and killed anyone who possessed them.
4. Took Yahweh's name out of the Scriptures, the only name for salvation, and filled the Scriptures with all kinds of pagan deity names and words from paganism.
5. Took the truth of Scriptures and made them a lie, mostly by putting pagan deity names and words into Scriptures to make them more acceptable to the pagan culture and to the uneducated masses to come over to Christianity.
6. Put Scriptures in a language the common and uneducated did not know, Latin, and taught it.
7. Had people who did not embrace Christianity killed because it was the only religion allowed at that time.
8. Constantine and many persecutors (before and after him) had burned many books to hide the truth.
9. All books were rewritten during the Dark Ages and they were manipulated. The impact of these actions is also reflected in history – as it had been altered from what it really was. The Papacy has altered the histories of numerous countries in an effort to conceal what some perceive as the Christian deception. Even the authenticity of the scriptures has been challenged and manipulated. Pagan Rome, through its adoption of Christianity, transformed the Scriptures into the proclaimed "Word of

God," thereby overshadowing what is considered the "Word of Yahweh." This act is seen by some as nullifying the potential for salvation within the Scriptures, and those who hold this view assert that the Papacy is aware of this contradiction.

Yahweh's Elect were never Christians, and this is proven by scriptures and history. Paul was never a pagan Christian or any of the other believers in Yahweh Messiah. THE BOOK OF CLEMENTS IS A LIE OF ROME. THEY HAVE MADE A LOT OF THEIR OWN CORRUPTED BOOKS TO TRY TO PASS THEM OFF AS ORIGINAL BOOKS FOR THEIR BENEFIT.

HE STARTED CHRISTIANITY FROM AN ALREADY EXISTING PAGAN RELIGION BY THE SAME NAME.

When Constantine started Christianity, the Roman Empire engulfed all the habitation of mankind. Look at a map at that time. Every culture had its own pagan religions. They were different in many of their practices. Christianity absorbed all of them. You had sun worshipers, moon worshipers, star worshipers, and every type of pagan deity imaginable; they worshiped nature and not the Creator.

Then the Reformation came, and people thought it was just the Christians starting their own denominations to get out from under the Pope's authority. Don't you realize that is how the pagan religions all started again also and how they got to start the Catholic denomination for more deceit?

So, Christianity has to go back to the days when Constantine created Christianity to be without denominations, and it will be made the RELIGION OF THE WORLD, like CONSTANTINE MADE IT THE UNIVERSAL STATE RELIGION OF THE ROMAN EMPIRE, FOR PEOPLE, THE ROMAN EMPIRE ENGULFED ALL THE PEOPLE AT

THAT TIME. It all must be re-lived, just like the book of Acts will be re-lived. History is going to repeat itself.

And power was given unto them (emperors) over the fourth part of the earth, (all of humanity) to kill with sword, and with hunger, and with death, and with the beasts of the earth.

Constantine used "Catholic" for what it means - UNIVERSAL - for his pagan, Satanic Christianity, making it Catholic in the sense of Universal when he declared Christianity the Universal religion of the Roman Empire because, at that time, the Roman Empire engulfed the whole of humanity. He enforced this by disallowing any other religion under the threat of death.

We are still living in the era of the Roman Empire, with the Popes taking the place of the emperors. Constantine created Christianity not to save people from the Lake of Fire but to ensure they ended up there. The name "Jesus Christ" cannot save a flea; Yahweh is the Messiah's name, the only name given for salvation, and there is no salvation available today. Yahweh has everyone covered, whether living or dead, to have the opportunity for salvation.

The Catholic denomination in Christianity did not exist before 1559 at the Council of Trent. The Jesuits controlled the education system and started the Universities, guided by the maxim, "Give me the child for the first seven years, and I'll give you the man." They understand that when children are brainwashed during their childhood, it shapes their beliefs. Constantine started Christianity from an already existing pagan religion by the same name.

History, thanks to the Jesuits and Papacy teaches that there were only 10 Roman Emperor Persecutions when there were eleven, and Constantine initiated the eleventh and last one that killed off the last of the Elect of Yahweh Messiah. All that was left on this earth were the pagans, and Constantine aimed to unify them under one heading,

Christianity, explaining why it is pagan to the core. Christians are often deceived, but only those who genuinely seek the truth will find it.

God is not only a sun deity but also a moon deity, which is the reason they say Allah means God, associating it with a moon deity like SIN.

Romans 1:25: "Who changed the truth of Yahweh into a lie, and worshipped and served the creature more than the Creator, who is blessed forever."

Constantine was the individual responsible for translating the Word of Yahweh from Hebrew into Greek, a fact easily proven. He then propagandized it. Subsequently, Jerome translated these works into Latin, and Erasmus, in turn, translated Jerome's Latin back into Greek, what is now referred to as the original Greek, to conceal Constantine's actions. This truth is seldom taught by institutions like the Christian apologists. My best advice to you and all Christians is to distance yourselves completely. The complete truth will emerge one last time, providing an opportunity for salvation.

Those who have died since Constantine up to the coming Papacy's 7-year Peace Plan, Daniel 8:25 And through his policy also he shall cause craft to prosper in his hand; and he shall magnify himself in his heart, and by peace shall destroy many: he shall also stand up against the King of Kings; but he shall be broken without hand, those Yahweh will teach during His Millennial Kingdom. WW3 is about to start at any time and will kill off 1/3 of the world's population, around 2.5 billion people.

The seven planets were considered the cosmos, and they were referred to as universal. The term "Catholic," meaning universal, originated from astrology rather than from the Christian Church (Vance, page 8).

1. He was the first Pope/Pontifex Maximus over Christianity, though Nimrod was the first to hold that title. Nimrod initiated paganism.
2. Constantine translated the Word of Yahweh from the original Hebrew into Greek.
3. He was the one who named the New Covenant the New Testament.
4. Constantine altered both the Roman 8-day calendar and the Hebrew 7-day week/New Moon calendar.
5. This world entirely became Satan's under Constantine.

TOTALLY SATAN'S WORLD

Satan was kicked out of heaven when the Messiah went back.

This is what caused the world to go out of whack.

The generations have been in Satan's world all this time,

The reason for wars, famine, disease, poverty, death, and crime.

Happening in the days of Peter and Paul

And how the believers fulfilled their call.

The fifth Seal was opened and showed they were all dead,

Waiting for the future believers, to their death, will also be led.

We are of the "Fifth Seal" generation that Rome has bred,

And into paganism, this world was led.

Away from the truth and into Satan's lies,

Making the scriptures void of salvation where everyone dies.

Christians do not realize the lie was already perpetuated,

Before the Reformation's cause was segregated.

The Papacy's World Empire is soon to be,

The Pope wants men in bondage and not free.

Yahweh's truth will come first where man can be forgiven,

Then, the Mark of the Beast, a Christian symbol, will be driven.

A famine of Yahweh's Word,

Where the truth was no longer heard.

By Gary W. Stanfield

STUDY ON BISHOPS: YAHWEH DID AWAY WITH JUDAISM.

Judaism had elders and priests, not bishops or deacons. The term "elder" comes from the Greek word "presbyteros," meaning "elder" or "old man." It refers to the ancient elders of Judaea who assisted Aaron and Moses in leading the children of Judaea. The word evolved into Latin as "presbyterus" and then into English as "presbyter," which was later shortened to "prester" and finally "priest."

In the days of the 11 Roman persecutions, when Yahweh's Assemblies existed, there was no such thing as the offices of bishop, priest, elder, or deacon. The assemblies met in one another's homes, and the Spirit was the overseer; no other individuals held official titles. Yahweh emphasized in Matthew 18:20, "For where two or three are gathered together in my name, there am I in the midst of them."

Examining Philippians 1:1, "Paul and Timotheus, the servants of Yahweh Messiah, to all the elect in Messiah Yahweh which is at Philippi, [with the bishops and deacons:]" note that the phrase "with the bishops and deacons" was added. The early assemblies did not have official titles, and this addition reflects a later development in the organizational structure of Christian communities.

With the following of 1 Timothy 3 chapter, that information cannot be true because the Spirit-filled were the elect of Yahweh and disciples of Yahweh. They needed no man to teach them.

1 John 2:27. But the anointing which ye have received of Him abideth in you, and ye need not that any man teach you: But as the same anointing teacheth you all things, and is truth, and is not lie, and even as it has taught you, ye shall abide in Him.

CONSTANTINE STARTED THE OFFICE OF BISHOP.

DEACONS, ELDERS, AND PASTORS ARE ALSO ROMAN LIES; THEY ARE LATER ADD-ONS.

Deacon is used in Catholic, Anglican, and Orthodox Christianity.

1 Timothy chapter 3 seems to be all made-up and messed with to push their lies for more deceit.

1 Timothy 3:1

¹ This is a true saying, if a man DESIRES THE OFFICE OF BISHOP, he desireth a good work.

² A bishop then must be blameless, the husband of one wife, vigilant, sober, of good behavior, given to hospitality, apt to teach;

³ Not given to wine, no striker, not greedy of filthy lucre; but patient, not a brawler, not covetous;

⁴ One that ruleth well his own house, having his children in subjection with all gravity;

⁵ (For if a man know not how to rule his own house, how shall he take care of the assembly of Yahweh?)

⁶ Not a novice, lest being lifted up with pride he falls into the condemnation of the devil.

⁷ Moreover he must have a good report of them which are without; lest he fall into reproach and the snare of the devil.

⁸ Likewise must the deacons be grave, not double tongued, not given to much wine, not greedy of filthy lucre;

⁹ Holding the mystery of the faith in a pure conscience.

¹⁰ And let these also first be proved; then let them use the office of a deacon, being found blameless.

¹¹ Even so must their wives be grave, not slanderers, sober, faithful in all things.

¹² Let the DEACONS be the husbands of one wife, ruling their children and their own houses well.

¹³ For they that have used the office of a deacon well purchase to themselves a good degree, and great boldness in the faith which is in Yahweh Messiah.

¹⁴ These things write I unto thee, hoping to come unto thee shortly:

¹⁵ But if I tarry long, that thou mayest know how thou ought to behave thyself in the House of Yahweh, which is the assembly of the living Yahweh, the pillar and ground of the truth.

¹⁶ And without controversy great is the mystery of righteousness: Yahweh was manifest in the flesh, justified in the Spirit, seen of Messengers, taught unto the Gentiles, believed on in the world, received up into heaven.

Verses 1-13 appear to be made up, and it is reasonable to believe that they were added later. 1 Corinthians 3:16-17

¹⁶ Know ye not that ye are the House of Yahweh, and that the Spirit of Yahweh dwelleth in you?

¹⁷ If any man defile the House of Yahweh, Him shall Yahweh destroy; for the House of Yahweh is righteous, which House ye are.

1 John 3:9 Whosoever is born of Yahweh doth not commit transgressions; for *His seed remaineth in* him: and he cannot transgress, because he is born of Yahweh.

Ephesians 4:11 "And he gave some, apostles; and some, prophets; and some teachers;"

1 Corinthians 12:1-13

¹ Now concerning spiritual gifts, brethren, I would not have you ignorant.

2 Ye know that ye were Gentiles, carried away unto these dumb idols, even as ye were led.

3 Wherefore I give you to understand, that no man speaking by the Spirit of Yahweh calleth Immanuel accursed: and that no man can say that Immanuel is Yahweh, but by the Spirit.

4 Now there are diversities of gifts, but the same Spirit.

5 And there are differences of administrations, but the same Spirit.

6 And there are diversities of operations, but it is the same Spirit which worketh all in all.

7 But the manifestation of the Spirit is given to every man to profit withal.

8 For to one is given by the Spirit the word of wisdom; to another the word of knowledge by the same Spirit;

9 To another faith by the same Spirit; to another the gifts of healing by the same Spirit;

10 To another the working of miracles; to another prophecy; to another discerning of spirits; to another diver's kinds of tongues; to another the interpretation of tongues:

11 But all these worketh that one and the selfsame Spirit, dividing to every man severally as he will.

12 For as the body is one, and hath many members, and all the members of that one body, being many, are one body: so also, is Yahweh.

13 For by one Spirit are we all baptized into one body, whether we be Jews or Gentiles, whether we be bond or free; and have been all made to drink into one Spirit.

CHAPTER 6
IF HIS BIRTH GIVEN NAME WAS NOT JESUS, WHAT WAS IT THEN?

THE NAME IMMANUEL IS HIS BIRTH NAME:

Matthew 13:55-56

55 Is not this the carpenter's son? Is not his mother called Mary? And his brethren, Jacob, and Joseph, and Simon, and Judah?

56 And his sisters, are they not all with us? Whence then hath this man all these things?

Mark 6:3 Is not this the carpenter, the son of Mary, the brother of Jacob, and Joseph, and of Judah, and Simon? And are not his sisters here with us? And they were offended at him.

KING JAMES RENAMED THE BOOK OF JACOB TO JAMES, AFTER HIMSELF.

Latin Vulgate has Jacob; Douay Rheims has James; King James has James, even though Jerome's Latin Vulgate was the root of it. The Douay Rheims was Jerome's Latin Vulgate put into the English, yet it has James. Why would the Catholics use James instead of Jacob in the Douay Rheims? It is another twisted Roman lie. Jacob is the real name of the book and his brother. This is the very reason they say James is another name for Jacob, which is nothing but a cover-up.

Jacob, Joseph, Judah, and Simon, the names of his brothers, are all Hebrew names, and Immanuel is also a Hebrew name, but Jesus is a Latinized Greek name. Why would Mary and Joseph give Hebrew names to all the other sons but name him JESUS? The answer is they would not. Immanuel was his birth-given name.

John 6:42 And they said, Is not this (Immanuel), the son of Joseph, whose father and mother we know? How is it then that he says, I came down from heaven?

You may be saying in my scriptures John 6:42 has the name Jesus or Yahshua and not Immanuel. Let me prove to you that Immanuel was his name.

Immanuel was prophesied in Isaiah 7:14 to be the name at birth. Everyone who knew him while growing up called him Immanuel. This was his earthly name, which would have been on the tax lists.

Isaiah 7:14 Therefore Yahweh himself shall give you a sign; Behold, a virgin shall conceive, and bear a son, and shall call his name Immanuel.

Isaiah 7:14 is the prophecy for Immanuel's name. Let's compare this with when the Messenger appeared to Joseph in a dream, telling him what to name the child. You will see the contradiction.

Matthew 1:23 is the fulfillment of the Isaiah 7:14 prophecy. Matthew 1:21-23 – THE LIE:

[21] And she shall bring forth a son, and thou shalt call his name JESUS: for he shall save his people from their sin. How the scripture should read: Matthew 1:21-23 – THE TRUTH:

[21] And she shall bring forth a son, and thou shalt call his name IMMANUEL: for he shall save his people from their transgressions.

[22] Now all this was done, to fulfill which was spoken of Yahweh by the prophet saying,

[23] Behold a virgin, young woman, shall be with child, and shall bring forth a son, and they shall call his name IMMANUEL, which being interpreted is Yahweh with us.

Luke 1:13 But the MESSENGER said unto him, Fear not, Zacharias: for thy prayer is heard; and thy wife Elisabeth shall bear thee a son, and THOU SHALT CALL HIS NAME JOHN.

Genesis 16:11 And the angel/MESSENGER of YAHWEH said unto her, Behold, thou art with child, and shalt bear a son, AND SHALT CALL HIS NAME ISHMAEL; because YAHWEH hath heard thy affliction.

Genesis 17:19 And Yahweh said, Sarah thy wife shall bear thee a son indeed; AND THOU SHALT CALL HIS NAME ISAAC: and I will establish my covenant with him for an everlasting covenant, and with his seed after him.

NOTICE: HOW THEY WERE TOLD BY THE MESSENGER TO NAME THEIR BABIES IMMANUEL, JOHN, ISHMAEL, AND ISAAC, BUT IMMANUEL WAS CHANGED TO JESUS, AND THE REST KEPT THE NAMES THEY WERE GIVEN AT BIRTH. THIS WAS ALL DONE TO DECEIVE THE WORLD WITH THE PAGAN NAME OF JESUS. As you should be able to see in the above verses, they put JESUS, SIN, LORD, AND GOD. These have all been proven to be pagan deity names. They inserted those into the scriptures to replace the true names or words, as you can observe, with the truth restored.

Matthew 1:21-23 – THE LIE:

21 And she shall bring forth a son, and thou shalt call his name JESUS: for he shall save his people from their sins.

How the scripture should read: Matthew 1:21-23 – THE TRUTH:

21 And she shall bring forth a son, and thou shalt call his name IMMANUEL: for he shall save his people from their transgressions.

22 Now all this was done, to fulfill which was spoken of Yahweh by the prophet saying,

23 Behold a virgin shall be with child, and shall bring forth a son, and they shall call his name IMMANUEL, which being interpreted is Yahweh with us.

24 Then Joseph being raised from sleep did as the Messenger of Yahweh had bidden him, and took unto him his wife:

25 And knew her not till she had brought forth her firstborn son: and he called his name IMMANUEL.

Isaiah 7:14 Behold, a virgin shall conceive, and bear a son, and shall call his name Immanuel.

PROPHECY

Matthew 1:23 Behold a virgin shall be with child, and shall bring forth a son, and they shall call his name IMMANUEL.

FULFILLMENT

The prophecy could never have been fulfilled if the birth-given name was any other than IMMANUEL. El means mighty one.

Isaiah 44:6 Thus says Yahweh the King of Judaea, and his redeemer Yahweh of hosts; I am the first, and I am the last; and beside me there is no EL/MIGHTY ONE. This is why EL at the end of IMMANUEL means YAHWEH WITH US, because there is no other except HIM.

Isaiah 8:8,10

[8] And he shall pass through Judaea; he shall overflow and go over, he shall reach even to the neck; and the stretching out of his wings shall fill the breadth of thy land, O Immanuel.

[10] Take counsel together, and it shall come to nought; speak the word, and it shall not stand: for Yahweh is with us.

THE PARADOX

Yahweh said his name would be Immanuel, NOT JESUS, NOT YAHSHUA, OR ANY OTHER NAME. The name Jesus is supposed to be a transliteration of the name Joshua or Yahshua. Let me now prove that Joshua and Jesus' names are not and were never the same name.

"Jesus" is the English equivalent of "Iesous" in Greek and "Iesus" in Latin. Notably, there is no direct equivalent in Hebrew for the name "Jesus."

On the other hand, "Joshua" is the English rendering, "IOSIAS" in Greek (ΙΟΣΙΑΣ), "Josue" in Latin, and "Yahshua" in Hebrew, meaning "Yahweh salvation."

The above is Joshua in English, Greek, Latin, and Hebrew. These next two verses are where they injected Jesus.

Hebrews 4:8 KJV: For if JESUS had given them rest, then would he not afterward have spoken of another day?

Hebrews 4:8 New American Standard Version: For if JOSHUA had given them rest, He would not have spoken of another day after that.

ACTS 10:36-37

36 The word which Yahweh sent unto the children of Judaea, teaching peace / THE WORD by YAHWEH MESSIAH (he is MASTER OF ALL:)

37 That word, I say, ye know, which was published throughout all Judaea, and began from Galilee, after the baptism which John taught.

Acts 6:7 *And the* Word of Yahweh increased.*"*

Acts 12:24 "*But the* Word of Yahweh grew and multiplied.*"*

Acts 13:49 "*And the Word of Yahweh was published throughout all the region.*"

Acts 19:20 "*So mightily grew the Word of Yahweh and prevailed.*" *It's all getting ready to happen once again.*

Luke 16:16 "The law and the prophets were until John: since that time the kingdom of Yahweh is taught, and every man presseth into it."

Galatians 1:6-7

[6] I marvel that ye are so soon removed from him that called you into the kingdom of Yahweh unto another Word:

[7] Which is not another; but there be some that trouble you and would pervert the Word of Yahweh.

CHAPTER 7
ARK OF THE COVENANT

The Ark of the Covenant is in heaven. The Ark of the Covenant could only be carried by Levite priests. WITH THE DESTRUCTION OF THE HOUSE OF YAHWEH IN 70 C.E., There was no more need for the Levites, and this was another reason for no longer having them. They carried the Ark by using two wooden poles inserted through rings on its sides, as touching the Ark itself would result in death at the hands of Yahweh. According to the Second Book of Samuel, the Levite Uzzah touched the Ark with his hand to steady it, and Yahweh instantly killed him.

Revelation 11:19 "And the HOUSE OF YAHWEH was opened in heaven, and there was seen in his House the Ark of his COVENANT: and there were lightnings, and voices, and thundering's, and an earthquake, and great hail."

IT WAS THROUGH CONSTANTINE THAT THE ARK OF THE COVENANT WAS CHANGED TO READ THE ARK OF THE TESTAMENT. CONSTANTINE ALSO CHANGED THE HOUSE OF YAHWEH TO TEMPLE since he was a pagan sun worshiper, and sun worshipers used Temples. Jews used the House of Yahweh. Jerome made the Old Covenant a lie by propagandizing it as you will be able to see in the next verses. YOU MUST REMEMBER Christianity HAS ALWAYS BEEN A PAGAN RELIGION AND WHY Constantine DID WHAT HE DID TO THE WORD OF Yahweh TO FURTHER HIS PAGAN RELIGION AND MASK IT ACCEPTABLE TO THE PAGANS.

1 Samuel 6:19 "And he smote the men of Bethshemesh, because they had looked into the Ark of the L/RD/YAHWEH, even he smote of the people fifty thousand and threescore and ten men: and the people lamented, because the L/RD/YAHWEH had smitten many of the people with a great slaughter."

Exodus 24:8 KJV And Moses took the blood, and sprinkled it on the people, and said, Behold the blood of the covenant, which YAHWEH hath made with you concerning all these words.

2 Samuel 6: 2-4; 10-13; 15-17

2 And David arose and went with all the people that were with him from Baale of Judah, to bring up from thence the Ark of YAHWEH, whose name is called by the name of YAHWEH of hosts that dwelleth between the cherubim's.

3 And they set the ark of YAHWEH upon a new cart and brought it out of the house of Abinadab that was in Gibeah: and Uzzah and Ahio, the sons of Abinadab, drove the new cart.

4 And they brought it out of the house of Abinadab which was at Gibeah, accompanying the Ark of YAHWEH: and Ahio went before the ark.

10 So David would not remove the Ark of YAHWEH unto him into the city of David: but David carried it aside into the house of Obededom the Gittite.

11 And the Ark of YAHWEH continued in the house of Obededom the Gittite three months: and Yahweh blessed Obededom, and all his household.

12 And it was told king David, saying, YAHWEH hath blessed the house of Obededom, and all that pertaineth unto him, because of the Ark of YAHWEH. So, David went and brought up the ark of Yahweh from the house of Obededom into the city of David with gladness.

13 And it was so, that when they that bare the ark of Yahweh HAD GONE SIX PACES, HE SACRIFICED OXEN AND FATLINGS.

15 So David and all the house of Israel brought up the Ark of YAHWEH with shouting, and with the sound of the trumpet.

16 And as the ark of Yahweh came into the city of David, Michal Saul's daughter looked through a window, and saw king David leaping and dancing before Yahweh; and she despised him in her heart.

17 And they brought in the Ark of YAHWEH, and set it in his place, in the midst of the tabernacle that David had pitched for it: and David offered burnt offerings and peace offerings before Yahweh.

CHAPTER 8
THE PAPACY STARTED BY CONSTANTINE IS OUT TO RULE THE WORLD AND WILL

"Furthermore, we declare, we proclaim, we define that it is absolutely necessary for salvation that every human creature be subject to the Roman Pontiff." (Declaratio quod subesse Romano Pontifici est omni humanae creaturae de necessitate salutis)

"Even if the Pope were Satan incarnate, we ought not to raise up our heads against him but calmly lie down to rest on his bosom. He who rebels against our Father is condemned to death, for that which we do to him we do to Christ: we honor Christ if we honor the Pope; we dishonor Christ if we dishonor the Pope (St. Catherine of Siena, SCS, p. 201-202, p. 222, quoted in Apostolic Digest, by Michael Malone,

Book 5: "The Book of Obedience", Chapter 1: "There is No Salvation Without Personal Submission to the Pope").

Ignatius Loyola himself declared the purpose of the Order was to: ". . . win to God [the Pope of Rome], not only a single nation, a single country but all nations, all the kingdoms of the world."

THE END TIME WORLD ORDER STARTS FROM 10 WORLD UNIONS THAT GIVE THEIR POWER TO THE POPE.

Revelation 6:7-8

And when he had opened the fourth seal, I heard the voice of the fourth beast say, Come and see. And I looked and behold a pale horse: and his name that sat on him was Death, and the grave followed with him. (emperor) And power was given unto them (emperors) over the fourth part of the earth, (all of humanity) to kill with sword, and with hunger, and with death, and with the beasts of the earth.

MAN OF TRANSGRESSIONS:

1 Thessalonians 2:1-16

¹ Now we beseech you, brethren, by the coming of our Master Yahweh Messiah, and by our gathering together unto Him,

² That ye be not soon shaken in mind, or be troubled, neither by spirit, nor by word, nor by letter as from us, as that the day of Yahweh is at hand.

³ Let no man beguile you in any wise; for, except the falling away come first, and the man of transgression be revealed the son of perdition,

⁴ He that opposes and exalts himself against all that is called a deity or that is worshipped; so that he sits in the temple of a deity, setting himself forth as a deity.

NOTE: It will not be the House of Yahweh that the Pope sits in. It will be the Temple of God inside the façade of the Dome of the Rock, which was built by Constantine, which was its name in the first

GARY WENDELL STANFIELD SR.

place. That's what Constantine named it when he built it in the 4th century. Yahweh did away with House of Yahweh worship and animal offerings, Levite priesthood, tithing, and what we call Judaism. So, there is no need for a House of Yahweh as far as Yahweh is concerned. He will build a new one during the Millennial Kingdom, the 3rd one.

5 Don't you remember, that, when I was yet with you, I told you these things?

6 And now you know that which restrains, to the end that he (Pontifex Maximus) may be revealed in his own season.

WHEN CONSTANTINE KILLED THE LAST ELECT PERSON, THAT IS WHEN YAHWEH TOOK HIS SPIRIT OF SALVATION FROM THIS EARTH.

7 For the mystery of lawlessness already works: only there is one that restrains now (the Spirit), until he be taken out of the way.

8 And then shall that Wicked be revealed, whom Yahweh shall consume with the spirit of his mouth, and shall destroy with the brightness of His coming:

9 Even him (POPE), whose coming is after the working of Satan with all power and signs and lying wonders,

10 And with all deceivableness of unrighteousness in them that perish; because they received not the love of the truth, that they might be saved.

Yahweh's salvation through the infilling of the Spirit is what let the Elect persevere the persecution and death where no pain was felt, and they had no fear during these tumultuous times.

11 And for this cause Yahweh shall send them strong delusion, that they should believe a lie:

12 That they all might be damned who believed not the truth but had pleasure in unrighteousness.

13 But we are bound to give thanks always to Yahweh for you, brethren beloved of Yahweh, because Yahweh hath from the beginning chosen you to salvation through the infilling of the Spirit and belief of the truth:

14 Whereunto he called you by our word, to the obtaining of the Spirit of our Master Yahweh Messiah.

15 Therefore, brethren, stand fast, and hold the traditions/truth which ye have been taught, whether by word, or our epistle/letter.

16 Now our Master Yahweh Messiah Himself, and Yahweh, even our Father, which hath loved us, and hath given us everlasting consolation and good hope through the Spirit,

1 John 2:18 Little children, it is the last time: and as ye have heard that anti-Messiah shall come, even now are there many anti-messiahs; whereby we know that it is the last time.

The spirit filled knew the truth because Yahweh taught His elect all things where no man needed to teach them, but there were many that believed the truth that were not yet filled with the Spirit of Yahweh.

1 Thessalonians 3:1-8, 14-15

1 Therefore, when we could endure it no longer, we thought it best to be left behind at Athens alone,

71

2 and we sent Timothy, our brother and Yahweh's fellow worker in the truth of the Messiah, to strengthen and encourage you as to your faith,

3 so that no one would be disturbed by these afflictions; for you yourselves know that we have been destined for this.

4 For indeed when we were with you, we kept telling you in advance that we were going to suffer affliction; and so it came to pass, as you know.

5 For this reason, when I could endure it no longer, I also sent to find out about your faith, for fear that the tempter might have tempted you, and our labor would be in vain.

6 But now that Timothy has come to us from you, and has brought us good news of your faith and love, and that you always think kindly of us, longing to see us just as we also long to see you,

7 for this reason, in all our distress and affliction we were comforted about you through your faith;

8 For now, we really live, if you stand firm in Yahweh.

14 "For you, brethren, became imitators of the assemblies of Yahweh in Messiah Yahweh that are in Judaea, for you also endured the same sufferings at the hands of your own countrymen, even as they did from the Jews,"

15 "who both killed the Messiah and the prophets and drove us out. They are not pleasing to Yahweh, but hostile to all men,

Life and Letters of St. Paul by David Smith, no copyright but ca. 1930 - Page 178, 179.

That imagination of Jewish eschatology was familiar to Paul's mind, and it furnished him with a cogent argument against the excesses of the Thessalonian enthusiasts. The Second Advent was indeed imminent.

The glorious consummation was at hand, but it would not immediately arrive. It would be heralded by two world-shaking preliminaries-- the dissolution of the Roman Empire and the appearance of the Anti-Messiah; and neither of these had yet come to pass.

The Little Horn of Daniel 7:25 would come from the Roman Empire, and then it would be changed, for this Little Horn or Anti-Messiah [Constantine] would change it to a religious government. This personage is no other than the Pope. The Pope is the only one who fulfills all the prophecies of the Anti-Messiah and Beast. The Roman Empire was changed over to a religious government, and the Papacy as a religious government could not come into existence until Constantine changed it from Secular over Religious power to Religious over Secular power.

Luke 24:47-49

47 And that repentance and remission of Transgressions should be taught in his name among all nations, beginning at Zion.

48 And ye are witnesses of these things.

49 And, behold, I send the promise of my Father upon you: but tarry ye in the city of Zion, until ye be endued with power from on high.

Acts 1:4,5,8

4 And, being assembled with them, commanded them that they should not depart from Zion, but wait for the promise of the Father, which, saith he, ye have heard of me.

⁵ For John truly baptized with water; but ye shall be baptized with the Spirit not many days hence.

⁸ But ye shall receive power, after that the Spirit is come upon you: and ye shall be witnesses unto me both in Zion, and in all Judea, and in Samaria, and unto the uttermost part of the earth.

Matt. 28:19 Go ye therefore, and teach all nations, baptizing them in the name of the Father, and of the Son, and of the Spirit (Yahweh):

Mark 16:15-20

¹⁵ And he said unto them, Go ye into all the world, and teach the Word to every creature.

¹⁶ He that believeth and is baptized shall be saved; but he that believeth not shall be damned.

¹⁷ And these signs shall follow them that believe; In my name shall they cast out devils; they shall speak with new tongues;

¹⁸ They shall take up serpents; and if they drink any deadly thing, it shall not hurt them; they shall lay hands on the sick, and they shall recover.

¹⁹ So then after Yahweh had spoken unto them, he was received up into heaven, and sat on the right hand of Yahweh.

²⁰ And they went forth, and taught everywhere, Yahweh working with *them*, and confirming the word with signs following.

In the next verse, Paul says that the Word was taught to every creature under heaven. BACK THEN!

Mark 16:16 He that believeth and is baptized shall be saved; but he that believeth not shall be damned. You see, the entire world back then had a choice to BELIEVE or NOT TO BELIEVE our ANCESTORS

WERE THE ONES WHO DID NOT BELIEVE, AND WE INHERITED THEIR LIES. THE FALLING AWAY TOOK PLACE BACK THEN.

CHAPTER 9
THE FIFTH SEAL OPENED BY CONSTANTINE THAT WE ARE LIVING AT THE VERY END OF

Revelation 6:9-11

[9] And when he had opened the fifth seal, I saw under the table the souls of them that were slain for the Word of Yahweh and for the testimony which they held:

Notice: These believers were killed at the end of the Fourth Seal for their testimony, which they held. Constantine finished Yahweh's elect off in the 11th Emperor persecution, which opened the 5th Seal, and the 5th Seal is the rule of the Papacy. We are living at the very end of it as we see the Papacy regaining its power in these last days.

[10] And they cried with a loud voice, saying, how long, O Yahweh, righteous and true, doest thou not judge and avenge our blood on them that dwell on the earth?

[11] And white robes were given unto every one of them: and it was said unto them, that they should rest yet for a little season until their fellow servants also, and their brethren that should be killed as they were, should be fulfilled. [These are the 7-Year Peace Plan elect.]

Before YAHWEH returns, the TRUTH will be taught ONCE MORE to EVERY NATION in the WORLD. He will pour HIS SPIRIT out ON THOSE who will ACCEPT THE TRUTH, THEN YAHWEH COMETH.

You see, that is HOW CHRISTIANITY came into existence. To deceive the world with Anti-Messiah names and religious lies. The Anti-Messiah or the Pope is the head of Christianity.

The Beast is the Papacy. They started Islam, and Christianity is going to be the world religion under the Papacy. Jesus is the name used in Christianity, which is pagan to the core, not Yahweh. Do you teach Yahweh as the Messiah and Creator? NO! There is no Trinity. It comes from paganism. The name Israel is a lie, Jacob was named Judaea, the true name. The name Jerusalem is also a lie. The true name is Zion.

CHRISTIANITY is saying they are taking the truth now to the entire world. What so-called truth are they teaching? An anti-messiah one, in the name of Jesus, which is also an anti-Messiah name.

Yahweh, as the Messiah, will be taught to every nation in the world just before the coming of the Anti-Messiah, and just before he takes his power once again.

1 John 2:22-23

22 Who is a liar but he that denieth that Jesus is the Christ? He is antichrist, that denieth the Father and the Son.

23 Whosoever denieth the son, the same hath not the Father: he that acknowledgeth the Son hath the Father also.

Acts 18:28 For he mightily convinced the Jews, and that publicly, showing by the scriptures that Yahweh was the Messiah.

2 Thess. Ch. 2:11 And for this cause Yahweh sends them a working of error, that they should believe a lie:

A. Then the lie came, and we have inherited the lies of our forefathers.

Jeremiah 16:19 O Yahweh, my strength, and my stronghold, and my refuge in the day of affliction, to you shall the nations come from the ends of the earth, and shall say, our fathers have inherited nothing but lies, even vanity and things in which there is no profit.

2 Thess. 2:12 That they should all be judged who believed not the truth but had pleasure in unrighteousness.

The True Believers in Yahweh were killed off during the Roman Empire's 11 Emperor persecutions. That is when people were given the strong delusion to believe a lie because these were the people who did not receive the knowledge of the truth that they might be saved. It was our ancestors who did not believe back then, and why we inherited the lies of our ancestors. The Papacy has been killing people ever since.

Dragon gave him his POWER, his SEAT, and his GREAT AUTHORITY====> PONTIFEX MAXIMUS That is why Rome is called Satan's seat.

In 1825, Pope Leo XII issued a papal coin with the writings "SEDET SUPER UNIVERSUM," which means the "UNIVERSAL SEAT OF AUTHORITY OVER THE ENTIRE WORLD.

The Pope will regain his power and it will be over the entire world this time. The truth is coming one more time; be ready to receive it in Yahweh's Name only.

All the believers back then knew they were going to die for their testimony that Yahweh was true.

Romans 9:28 "For he will finish the work, and cut *it* short in righteousness: because a short work will Yahweh make upon the earth."

The Tribulation Period for those back then lasted 247 years; the coming future Tribulation Period will only last for 3 ½ years, now that is quick work! The great falling away happened back then.

The great falling happened during the 11 Roman Emperor persecutions. Christianity wants you to believe it did not happen back then but is a future thing, but it has already happened.

Before YAHWEH returns, the TRUTH will be taught ONCE MORE to EVERY NATION in the WORLD. He will pour HIS SPIRIT out ON THOSE who will ACCEPT THE TRUTH, THEN YAHWEH COMETH.

You see, that is HOW CHRISTIANITY came into existence. To deceive the world with Anti-Messiah names and religious lies. The Anti-Messiah or the Pope is the head of Christianity.

CHRISTIANITY is saying they are taking the truth now to the whole world. What so-called truth are they teaching? An anti-messiah one, in the name of Jesus, an anti-Messiah name.

Yahweh, as the Messiah, will be taught to every nation in the world just before the coming of the Anti-Messiah and just before he takes his power once again.

1 John 2:22-23

22 Who is a liar? but he that denies that Yahweh is the Messiah. He is Anti-Messiah, that denies the Father and the Son.

23 Whosoever denies the Son, the same has not the Father: {but} he that acknowledges the Son has the Father also.

Acts 18:28 For he mightily convinced the Jews, and that publicly, showing by the scriptures that Yahweh was the Messiah.

CHAPTER 10
THE LIE OF THE WORD "CHRISTIAN" IN ACTS 11:26; Acts 26:28 and 1 Peter 4:16

ACTS 11:26

Acts 11:26 and when he found him, he brought him to Antioch. So for a whole year Barnabas and Saul met with the assembly and taught great numbers of people. The disciples were called Christians / Judaeans. First at Antioch. (This is because this is when the first Gentiles were given salvation.)

This study is to prove that the word "JUDAEAN" WAS REPLACED WITH THE WORD "CHRISTIAN" BY Constantine AND HIS PAGAN BISHOPS. So, this is all about how a Gentile becomes a Judaean and not being a part of the bloodline. It is all about how Yahweh grafts a Gentile into the Judaean tree, where there is neither Jew nor Gentile, but all are made one, by the infilling of Yahweh's Spirit and the belief and faith in Yahweh Messiah.

Which will all be proven by scriptures.

This is why the Apostles were sent to the 12 tribes. Also, in:

1 Peter 4:16

16 Yet if any man suffer as a Christian/JUDAEAN, let him not be ashamed; but let him esteem Yahweh on this behalf.

Acts 26:28

[28] Then Agrippa said unto Paul, Almost thou persuadest me to be a Christian/JUDAEAN.

Ephesians 3:4-9

[4] Whereby, when ye read, ye may understand my knowledge in the mystery of Yahweh

[5] Which in other ages was not made known unto the sons of men, as it is now revealed unto his apostles and prophets by the Spirit;

[6] That the Gentiles should be fellow heirs, and of the same body, and partakers of his promise in Yahweh by the word:

[7] Whereof I was made a minister, according to the gift of the Spirit of Yahweh given unto me by the effectual working of his power.

[8] Unto me, who am less than the least of all the Elect, is this Spirit given, that I should teach among the Gentiles the unsearchable riches of Yahweh;

[9] And to make all men see what is the fellowship of the mystery, which from the beginning of the world hath been hid in Yahweh, who created all things by Yahweh Messiah:

1 Corinthians. 12:13 For by one Spirit are we all baptized into one body, whether *we be* Jews or Gentiles, whether *we be* bond or free; and have been all made to drink into one Spirit.

EPHESIANS 2:8, 11-15

[8] For by THE SPIRIT are ye saved through faith; and that not of yourselves: it is the gift of YAHWEH:

[11] Wherefore remember, that ye being in time past Gentiles in the flesh, who are called Uncircumcision by that which is called the Circumcision in the flesh made by hands;

12 That at that time ye were without YAHWEH, being aliens from the commonwealth of Judaea, and strangers from the covenants of promise, having no hope, and without YAHWEH in the world:

13 But now in MESSIAH YAHWEH ye who sometimes were far off are made nigh by the blood of THE MESSIAH.

14 For he is our salvation, who hath made both one, and hath broken down the middle wall of partition between us; (JEW AND GENTILE TO JUDAEAN)

15 Having abolished in his flesh the enmity, even the law of commandments contained in ordinances; for to make in himself of twain one new man, so making peace;

EPHESIANS 2:16-22

16 And that he might reconcile both unto YAHWEH in one body by the TREE, having slain the enmity thereby:

17 And came and taught SALVATION to you which were afar off, and to them that were nigh.

18 For through him we both have access by one Spirit unto the Father.

19 Now therefore ye are no more strangers and foreigners, but fellow citizens with the ELECT, and of the household of Yahweh;

20 And are built upon the foundation of the apostles and prophets, YAHWEH MESSIAH himself being the chief corner stone;

21 In whom all the building fitly framed together growth unto a righteous HOUSE in YAHWEH:

22 In whom ye also are builded together for an habitation of YAHWEH through the Spirit.

Romans 10:11-13

[11] For the scripture saith, Whosoever believeth on him shall not be ashamed.

[12] For there is no difference between the Jew and the Greek: for the same Yahweh over all is rich unto all that call upon him.

[13] For whosoever shall call upon the name of Yahweh shall be saved.

Colossians 3:9-11

[9] Lie not one to another, seeing that ye have put off the old man with his deeds;

[10] And have put on the new man, which is renewed in knowledge after the image of him that created him:

[11] Where there is neither Greek nor Jew, circumcision nor uncircumcision, Barbarian, Scythian, bond nor free: but YAHWEH is all, and in all.

Romans 11:16-24

[16] For if the first fruit (MESSIAH) be righteous, the lump is also righteous: and if the root be righteous, so are the branches.

[17] And if some of the branches be broken off, and thou, being a wild olive tree, wert grafted in among them, and with them partakest of the root and fatness of the olive tree;

[18] Boast not against the branches. But if thou boast, thou bearest not the root, but the root thee.

[19] Thou wilt say then, The branches were broken off, that I might be grafted in.

20 Well; because of unbelief they were broken off, and thou standest by faith. Be not high-minded, but fear:

21 For if YAHWEH spared not the natural branches, take heed lest he also spare not thee.

22 Behold therefore the goodness and severity of YAHWEH: on them which fell, severity; but toward thee, goodness, if thou continue in his goodness: otherwise thou also shalt be cut off.

23 And they also, if they abide not still in unbelief, shall be grafted in: for YAHWEH is able to graf t them in again.

24 For if thou wert cut out of the olive tree which is wild by nature, and wert grafted contrary to nature into a good olive tree: how much more shall these, which be the natural branches, be grafted into their own olive tree

Ephesians 3:6-7

6 That the Gentiles should be fellow heirs, and of the same body, and partakers of his promise in Yahweh by the WORD:

7 Whereof I was made a minister, according to the gift of the SPIRIT of YAHWEH given unto me by the effectual working of his power.

Galatians 3: 3-29

3 O foolish Galatians, who hath bewitched you, that ye should not obey the truth, before whose eyes YAHWEH MESSIAH hath been evidently set forth, KILLED among you?

2 This only would I learn of you, Received ye the Spirit by the works of the law, or by the hearing of faith?

3 Are ye so foolish? Having begun in the Spirit, are ye now made perfect by the flesh?

⁴ Have ye suffered so many things in vain? If it be yet in vain.

⁵ He therefore that ministereth to you the Spirit, and worketh miracles among you, doeth he it by the works of the law, or by the hearing of faith?

⁶ Even as Abraham believed Yahweh, and it was accounted to him for righteousness.

⁷ Know ye therefore that they which are of faith, the same are the children of Abraham.

⁸ And the scripture, foreseeing that YAHWEH would justify the heathen through faith, taught before the WORD unto Abraham, saying, In thee shall all nations be blessed.

⁹ So then they which be of faith are blessed with faithful Abraham.

¹⁰ For as many as are of the works of the law are under the curse: for it is written, Cursed is everyone that continueth not in all things which are written in the book of the law to do them.

¹¹ But that no man is justified by the law in the sight of YAHWEH, it is evident: for, The just shall live by faith.

¹² And the law is not of faith: but, The man that doeth them shall live in them.

¹³ YAHWEH hath redeemed us from the curse of the law, being made a curse for us: for it is written, Cursed is everyone that hangeth on a tree:

¹⁴ That the blessing of Abraham might come on the Gentiles through YAHWEH MESSIAH; that we might receive the promise of the Spirit through faith.

15 Brethren, I speak after the manner of men; Though it be but a man's covenant, yet if it be confirmed, no man disannulleth, or addeth thereto.

16 Now to Abraham and his seed were the promises made. He saith not, And to seeds, as of many; but as of one, And to thy seed, which is YAHWEH.

17 And this I say, that the covenant, that was confirmed before of YAHWEH in MESSIAH, the law, which was four hundred and thirty years after, cannot disannul, that it should make the promise of none effect.

18 For if the inheritance be of the law, it is no more of promise: but YAHWEH gave it to Abraham by promise.

19 Wherefore then serveth the law? It was added because of transgressions, till the seed should come to whom the promise was made; and it was ordained by MESSENGERS in the hand of a mediator.

20 Now a mediator is not a mediator of one, but YAHWEH is one.

21 Is the law then against the promises of YAHWEH? YAHWEH forbid: for if there had been a law given which could have given life, verily righteousness should have been by the law.

22 But the scripture hath concluded all under TRANSGRESSION, that the promise by faith of YAHWEH MESSIAH might be given to them that believe.

23 But before faith came, we were kept under the law, shut up unto the faith which should afterwards be revealed.

24 Wherefore the law was our schoolmaster to bring us unto YAHWEH, that we might be justified by faith.

25 But after that faith is come, we are no longer under a schoolmaster.

26 For ye are all the children of YAHWEH by faith in MESSIAH YAHWEH.

27 For as many of you as have been baptized into YAHWEH have put on YAHWEH.

28 There is neither Jew nor Greek, there is neither bond nor free, there is neither male nor female: for ye are all one in MESSIAH YAHWEH.

29 And if ye be YAHWEH'S, then are ye Abraham's seed, and heirs according to the PROMISE.

John 10:9 I am the door; if any one enters by me, he will be saved.

John 14:6 Immanuel said to him, "I am the way, and the truth, and the life; no one comes to the Father, but by me.

Hebrew 10:19-20 We have confidence to enter the sanctuary by the blood of Yahweh, by the new and living way which he opened for us through the curtain, that is, through his flesh.

Acts 4:12 Neither is there salvation in any other: for there is none other name under heaven given among men, whereby we must be saved.

Isaiah 2:2-3

2 In the last days the mountain of YAHWEH'S HOUSE will be established as the highest of the mountains; it will be exalted above the hills, and all nations will stream to it.

3 Many peoples will come and say, "Come, let us go up to the mountain of YAHWEH, to the HOUSE OF YAHWEH the ALMIGHTY

of JUDAEA. He will teach us his ways, so that we may walk in his paths." The law will go out from Zion, the Word of YAHWEH from Zion.

Ezekiel 47:21-23

21 "You are to distribute this land among yourselves according to the tribes of Judaea.

22 You are to allot it as an inheritance for yourselves and for the foreigners residing among you and who have children. You are to consider them as native-born Judaean; along with you they are to be allotted an inheritance among the tribes of Judaea.

23 In whatever tribe a foreigner resides, there you are to give them their inheritance," declares the Sovereign Yahweh.

CHAPTER 11
WHO ARE OF THE ASSEMBLY OF SATAN?

Romans 2:28-29

28 For he is not a Judaean, which is one outwardly; neither is that circumcision, which is outward in the flesh:

29 But he is a Judaean, which is one inwardly; and circumcision is that of the heart, in the spirit, and not in the letter; whose praise is not of men, but of Yahweh.

Revelation 3:9 Behold, I will make them of the synagogue/assembly of Satan, which say they are Judaeans, and are not, but do lie; behold, I will make them to come and worship before thy feet, and to know that I have loved thee.

Galatians 3:7 Therefore know that only those who are of faith are sons of Abraham.

SATAN KICKED OUT OF HEAVEN

Revelation 12:9 "And the great dragon was cast out, that old serpent, called the Devil, and Satan, which deceiveth the whole world: he was cast out into the earth, and his angels/messengers were cast out with him."

Luke 10:18 "I beheld Satan as lightning fall from heaven."

The only time in human history that Satan could deceive the whole world is from Constantine to the coming Papacy 7-Year Peace

Plan that will end WW3. Salvation will be available again during the 7-Year Peace Plan.

1 Thessalonians 2:11 And for this cause, Yahweh shall send them strong delusion, that they should believe a lie:

This totally became Satan's world under Constantine

TOTALLY SATAN'S WORLD

Satan was kicked out of heaven when the Messiah went back.

This is what caused the world to go out of whack.

The generations have been in Satan's world all this time,

The reason for wars, famine, disease, poverty, death, and crime.

Happening in the days of Peter and Paul

And how the believers fulfilled their call.

The fifth Seal was opened and showed they were all dead,

Waiting for the future believers, to their death, will also be led.

We are of the "Fifth Seal" generation that Rome has bred,

And into paganism, this world was led.

Away from the truth and into Satan's lies,

Making the scriptures void of salvation where everyone dies.

Christians do not realize the lie was already perpetuated,

Before the Reformation's cause was segregated.

The Papacy's World Empire is soon to be,

The Pope wants men in bondage and not free.

Yahweh's truth will come first where man can be forgiven,

Then, the Mark of the Beast, a Christian symbol, will be driven.

A famine of Yahweh's Word,

Where the truth was no longer heard.

By Gary W. Stanfield

CHAPTER 12
YAHWEH'S WORD HID

Amos 8:11-12

11 Behold, the days come, saith Yahweh, that I will send a famine in the land, not a famine of bread, nor a thirst for water, but of hearing the Words of Yahweh.

12 And they shall wander from sea to sea, and from the north even to the east, they shall run to and fro to seek the Word of Yahweh and shall not find it.

Romans 1:25 They exchanged the truth about Yahweh for a lie, and worshiped and served created things rather than the Creator-- who is forever praised. IT WAS OUR ANCESTORS WHO DID NOT BELIEVE IN THE DAYS OF PETER AND PAUL, AND WE INHERITED THEIR LIES.

Daniel 12:4 But thou, O Daniel, shut up the words, and seal the book, even to the time of the end: many shall run to and fro, and knowledge shall be increased.

Isaiah 60:1-3 1. Arise, shine; for thy light is come, and the righteousness of Yahweh is risen upon thee.

2 For, behold, the darkness shall cover the earth, and gross darkness the people: but Yahweh shall arise upon thee, and His righteousness shall be seen upon thee.

3 And the Gentiles shall come to Thy light, and kings to the brightness of Thy rising.

Isaiah 25:7

7: And He will destroy in this mountain the face of the covering cast over all people and the veil that is spread over all nations.

Romans 10:14 How then shall they call on Him in whom they have not believed? and how shall they believe in Him of whom they have not heard? and how shall they hear without a teacher?

Jeremiah 16:19 Yahweh, my strength, and my fortress, and my refuge in the day of affliction, the Gentiles shall come unto thee from the ends of the earth, and shall say, surely our fathers have inherited lies, vanity, and things wherein there is no profit.

Scriptures were made a lie by Constantine and Jerome. There are no originals unless the Vatican is sitting on them and why, through study people are trying to bring about more truth from them. The Roman Empire and the Roman Empire under Constantine and others had over one thousand years from 14, 25, or 40 generations of people, and that depends on how many years makes a generation, though; some say 70 years, 40 years, and 25 years, to perpetuate the lie of Jesus Christ too. The following is how it was done:

1. Mixed pagan religions, including Judaism = Christianity.
2. Added pagan holidays like Christmas and Easter to influence pagans to come over to Christianity.
3. Collected all existing manuscripts and had anyone killed who possessed them.
4. Took Yahweh's name out of the Scriptures, the only name for salvation, and filled the Scriptures with all kinds of pagan deity names and pagan words from paganism.
5. Took the truth of Scriptures and made them a lie, mostly by putting Pagan Deity names and words into Scriptures to make them more acceptable to the Pagan culture and to the uneducated masses to come over to Christianity.

6.   Put Scriptures in a language the common and uneducated did not know (Latin) and taught it.

7.   Have anyone who does not come over to Christianity killed because it was the only religion allowed at that time.

8.   Constantine and many persecutors before and after him had many book burnings to hide the truth.

9.   All books were rewritten during that time, and there were many forgeries; by doing this, they also changed history from what it really was. Christianity has changed the histories of many countries just to cover up the Christian lie. Even the truth of the Scriptures was made a lie. What Pagan Rome has done with their Christianity was to make the Scriptures the "Word of God," which made void the "Word of Yahweh," which makes the Scriptures void of salvation, and they know this.

CHAPTER 13
PAGAN HOLIDAYS CHRISTIANIZED:

Constantine Christianized pagan holidays like Christmas, Easter, Lent, and many others to make Christianity more appealing to the pagans; of late, they have even Christianized Halloween, the most Satanic of them all, it seems. In 325 C.E., At the Council of Nicaea, he changed the Passover for Easter, that Easter must be celebrated on Sunday and that Passover must be forbidden. Ensured Easter and Passover would never be on the same day. That is why Easter is in King James in Acts 12:4. This was all done to paganize his Christianity and has nothing to do with the faith of Yahweh but for deceiving the world with his Satanic lies.

CHRISTMAS - is the rebirth of all sun deities. TO NAME A FEW OF THEM, JESUS, CHRIST, LORD, GOD, ADONAI, SACRED, AMEN, BIBLE. This is why December 25, Nimrod's birthday, was picked for the birth date of the sun deity Jesus which was picked as the birth-given name by Constantine and his pagan bishops.

This should help to see how Christmas and Easter coincide with each other in pagan sun worship. From the re-birth of the sun to its resurrection in paganism. The Easter sunrise service—standing with their faces toward the east, as the sun is rising, in a service of worship that honors the sun god and his mythical idolatrous consort, goddess Easter.

This should help people see how Constantine went about falsifying the scriptures making them a pagan lie.

EASTER IS A PAGAN DEITY OF FERTILITY, AND WHY THEY HAVE THE RABBIT AND CHICKEN TO REPRESENT IT; BOTH ARE KNOWN FOR FERTILITY.

He also made Sunday the Christian Sabbath since it was the day that pagans worshiped the sun. Constantine instructed that Christians and non-Christians should be united in observing the "venerable day of the sun." Constantine even wore a crown with sunbursts.

CHRISTIANITY A PAGAN LIE

Christianity is the only one that will last,

It will absorb all the religions of the past.

It was created to be a pagan religious lie,

Making salvation void so that men die.

Adonai, Angel, Bible, Easter, Hell, Sin,

Jesus, Christ, Grace, Hades, God, Amen.

Also, Lord, is just another pagan name,

That was used to take Yahweh's fame.

Altar, cross, ghost, saint, gospel, trinity,

Church, hymn, hallowed, steeple, holy.

Pagan words used just to mislead man,

This was all done for Constantine's plan.

A famine of the Word was brought about.

Generations are why it was not figured out.

Crusades, Dark Ages, Inquisitions, all do tell,

The Reformation was used for people to rebel.

Not realizing, still under the same old roof,

They do not know the lies, without proof.

Yahweh is the Messiah's name for salvation,

The last day truth and a truth proclamation!

By Gary W. Stanfield

Constantine did away with anything to do with Judaism. This is the reason for Constantine's Apostle Creed.

He used Nimrod's birthday (December 25) as the birthday for their Jesus, which is a sun deity name, and he used many other ones in his propagandized scriptures, such as Lord, Christ, God, Amen, Adonai, Hell, Hades, and Sacred in later editions was also added to the Christian Pantheon of deity names from diverse cultures.

CHAPTER 14
IMMANUEL WAS BORN ON NISSAN 1ST

DURING THE FIRST DAY OF SPRING AND THE NEW YEAR.

This is a video by Jonathan Cahn (YouTube). While the studies in my book are all my own work, this video analysis of the Star of Bethlehem is by Jonathan Cahn. I've added my own explanation of what the star truly was, differing from Cahn's take.

Luke 2:8-14

8 And there were in the same country shepherds abiding in the field, keeping watch over their flock by night.

LAMBS ARE ONLY BORN IN THE SPRING, SO THEY ARE WATCHING FOR THE LAMBS BEING BORN AT NIGHT.

9 And, lo, the MESSENGER of YAHWEH came upon them, and the RIGHTEOUSNESS OF YAHWEH shone round about them: and they were sore afraid. A SPACECRAFT.

10 And the Messenger said unto them, Fear not: for, behold, I bring you good tidings of great joy, which shall be to all people.

11 For unto you is born this day in the city of David a Savior, which is MESSIAH YAHWEH.

12 And this shall be a sign unto you; Ye shall find the babe wrapped in swaddling clothes, lying in a manger.

13 And suddenly there was with the Messenger a multitude of the heavenly host praising YAHWEH, and saying,

14 RIGHTEOUSNESS to YAHWEH in the highest, and on earth peace, good will toward men.

IN THE SPRING SHEPHERDS WATCHED THE SHEEP AT NIGHT. LAMBS ARE BORN IN THE SPRING. THEY WATCH FOR THE LAMBS. THESE LAMBS ARE PASSOVER LAMB OFFERINGS, TO BE OFFERED AT THE PASSOVER, THE NEXT YEAR. SO, THEY WILL BE A MALE OF THE FIRST YEAR, SO IT DOES NOT HAVE TO BE A FULL YEAR OLD. WHEN THE PASSOVER COMES.

WHEN DOES THE JEWISH NEW YEAR START?

The National New Year: "This shall be the first of the months to you" (Exodus). Yahweh gives this command with respect to the month of Aviv/Nissan, the month when JUDAEA was freed from slavery in Egypt.

Nissan 1st (April) SPRING STARTS IN JUDAEA. ALSO NEW YEARS DAY, START ON SAME DAY.

EXODUS 12:2 This month shall be unto you the beginning of months: it shall be the first month of the year to you.

Exodus 12:5 Your lamb shall be without blemish, a male of the first year: ye shall take it out from the sheep, or from the goats:

THEY TAKE THE LAMBS TO THEIR HOMES ON THE 10TH OF NISSAN, WHICH COINCIDES WITH PALM SUNDAY, FOUR DAYS BEFORE PASSOVER.

Zion was crowded with pilgrims who had come for the annual Passover celebration. IMMANUEL rode into Zion on A donkey. THIS

WAS THE DAY THEY TOOK THE PASSOVER LAMB INTO THEIR HOUSES.

Exodus 12:3,6

3 Speak ye unto all the congregation of Judaea, saying, In the tenth day of this month they shall take to them every man a lamb, according to the house of their fathers, a lamb for a house:

6 And ye shall keep it up until the fourteenth day of the same month: and the whole assembly of the congregation of Judaea shall kill it in the evening.

Exodus 40:2 On the first day of the first month shalt thou set up the tabernacle of the tent of the congregation.

John 1:10 "He was in the world, and the world was made by him, and the world knew him not." HE TABERNACLED AMONG US.

THE ABOVE CAME FROM A VIDEO TEACHING BY JONATHAN CAHN. HE TEACHES THAT THE STAR WAS THE PLANET JUPITER AND ANOTHER ONE. THIS IS NOT TRUE; IT WAS A SPACECRAFT. HIS TEACHING IS VERY GOOD AND THOROUGH, THOUGH, ON THE SUBJECT OF THE TIME OF THE BIRTH OF THE STAR.

Let's start when the wise men came to Zion first. When they saw the star, they were taken to Zion, not Bethlehem, where Immanuel was born. This was done so Herod would fulfill the prophecy of killing all the male children 2 years old and younger. The wise men left Zion and went to Bethlehem to find Immanuel living in a house, not a manger, and he was 2 years old, not a baby.

Matthew 2:16-18

16 Then Herod, when he saw that he was mocked of the wise men, was exceeding wroth, and sent forth, and slew all the children that

were in Bethlehem, and in all the coasts thereof, from two years old and under, according to the time which he had diligently inquired of the wise men.

17 Then was fulfilled that which was spoken by Jeremiah the prophet, saying,

18 In Rama was there a voice heard, lamentation, and weeping, and great mourning, Rachel weeping for her children, and would not be comforted, because they are not.

THE FIRST 144,000

We must show that the Messiah was the first to be resurrected from the dead to everlasting life. Scriptures tell us He had to be the first.

Acts 26:23 That the Messiah should suffer, and that he should be the first that should rise from the dead, and should show light unto the people, and to the Gentiles.

1 Cor. 15:23 But every man in his own order: the Messiah, the firstfruits; afterward they that are the Messiah's at his coming.

Acts 10:40-41

[40] Him Yahweh raised up the third day, and shewed him openly;

[41] Not to all the people, but unto witnesses chosen before of Yahweh, even to us, who did eat and drink with him after he rose from the dead.

Yahweh is never without a witness.

Rev. 14:1-5

[1] And I looked, and lo, a Lamb stood on the Mount Zion, and with him an hundred forty and four thousand, having his Father's name written in their foreheads.

[2] And I heard a voice from heaven, as the voice of many waters, and as the voice of a great thunder: and I heard the voice of harpers harping with their harps.

[3] And they sung as it were a new song before the throne, and before the four beasts, and the elders: and no man could learn that song but the hundred and forty and four thousand, which were redeemed from the earth.

[4] These are they which were not defiled with women; for they are virgins. These are they which follow the Lamb withersoever he goeth. These were redeemed from among men, being the firstfruits unto the Father and to the Lamb.

[5] And in their mouth was found no guile: for they are without fault before the throne of Yahweh.

[1] Were not defiled with women; they were virgins = male babies.

[2] They follow the Lamb whithersoever he goeth.

³ They were redeemed from among men = already gone.

⁴ First Fruits unto the Father and to the Lamb = they were the first ones to obtain salvation, given credit to the Lamb.

ALL THIS HAPPENS DURING THE MONTH OF NISAN. THEY TAKE THE LAMB TO THEIR HOUSES ON SATURDAY, THE 10TH. IMMANUEL DIED ON THE FOLLOWING WEDNESDAY, THE 14TH, ON PASSOVER. THE NEXT DAY, THURSDAY, THE 15TH, WAS A SPECIAL SABBATH, THE FIRST DAY OF UNLEAVENED BREAD. FRIDAY, THE 16TH, WAS THE PREPARATION DAY FOR THE WEEKLY SABBATH ON SATURDAY, THE 17TH. IMMANUEL ROSE AT THE END OF THE 7TH-DAY SABBATH. THE 18TH WAS THE FEAST OF THE FIRST FRUITS.

⁵ In their mouth was found no guile = babies.

⁶ They were without fault = babies.

NOTICE: In verse 1, only the Lamb and the 144,000 are standing on Mount Zion. They were there to be redeemed from the earth, as verse 3 states.

The People's Bible Encyclopedia, page 1196, c. 1924:

ZION - The most southwestern hill and the highest in Zion. ...the summit of Zion was cut away in the age of the Maccabees in order that it might be overlooked by the House hill. Did Yahweh have this happen for His future use for the 144,000?

Compare this with when the Messiah returns the second time to set up His earthly kingdom in the following verses.

Zechariah 14:4 And his feet shall stand in that day upon the Mount of Olives, which is before Zion on the east, and the Mount of Olives shall cleave in the midst thereof toward the east and toward the west, and there shall be a very great valley; and half of the mountain shall remove toward the north, and half of it toward the south.

Also, let's look at Acts Ch. 1, verses 11 and 12, when the Messiah ascended into heaven, with his disciples looking on. (In a spacecraft.)

Acts 1:11-12

[11] Which also said, Ye men of Galilee, why stand ye gazing up into heaven? This same Messiah, which is taken up from you into heaven, shall so come in like manner as ye have seen him go into heaven.

So, he will return in a spacecraft with all his Messengers in their spacecraft coming with him, not riding horses like Christianity teaches. Horses cannot ride through space.

HE WENT UP IN A SPACECRAFT AND WILL RETURN IN ONE.

[12] Then returned they unto Zion from the mount called Olives, which is from Zion. A sabbath day's journey.

Notice that when He returns, He will return to the Mount of Olives, and at His Ascension from His disciples, it was from the Mount of Olives, not Mount Zion.

You must now see that verse 1 is talking about when the 144,000 were redeemed from the earth. They will be with Yahweh when He returns.

Notice in verses 2 and 3 of Revelation Ch. 14 that they show the heavenly scene after the redemption of these 144,000. When did this happen?

John 20:17 Immanuel saith unto her, Touch me not; for I am not yet ascended to my Father: but go to my brethren, and say unto them, I ascend unto my Father, and your Father; and to my Mighty One and your Mighty One.

Notice here that Immanuel told Mary not to touch him, for he had not ascended to the Father.

As you read John Ch. 20, you find Immanuel returns that same day in the evening to his disciples. He shows them his side. Eight days later, he returns to his disciples, and Thomas is with them this time. Since Thomas doubted, he had him touch his side. Notice that he had Thomas touch him, and he told Mary not to touch him. So it was between this time that he had ascended to the Father with the redeemed 144,000, or it happened when He went back for good. These babies' parents would still be living when they were resurrected, so He may have let them stay until His final departure and his soon return to the earth.

Matt. 27:51-53

51 And, behold, the veil of the House of Yahweh was rent in twain from the top to the bottom; and the earth did quake, and the rocks rent:

⁵² And the graves were opened; and many bodies of the believers which slept arose,

⁵³ And came out of the graves after his resurrection and went into the righteous city and appeared unto many.

There is a key point to be made here. Why were these raised after the Messiah was resurrected and not before when the graves were first opened? For the simple reason that they were to be raised to everlasting life. If they had been resurrected at the time of the first earthquake when the graves were opened, it would mean they would have had to die again, just like Lazarus. The Messiah had to be raised from the dead first to everlasting life. Many thought and even taught that the resurrection had already taken place because of the babies being resurrected.

2 Timothy 2:8 "Who concerning the truth have erred, saying that the resurrection is past already; and overthrow the faith of some."

The second earthquake happened when the Messenger rolled back the stone to the Messiah's tomb.

Matt. 28:2,6

² And, behold, there was a great earthquake: for the Messenger of Yahweh descended from heaven, and came and rolled back the stone from the door, and sat upon it.

⁶ He is not here: for he is risen, as he said. Come, see the place where Yahweh Messiah lay.

Let's go back to verses 4 and 5 of Revelation Ch. 14. Notice the following points made about these 144,000:

1. They were not defiled by women; they were virgins; they were all males.

2.   They were redeemed from among men.

3.   They follow the Messiah wherever he goes.

4.   They are without fault before the throne of Yahweh.

5.   The firstfruits unto the Father and to the Lamb. Who are they?

Matt. 2:16 Then Herod, when he saw that he was mocked of the wise men, was exceeding wroth, and sent forth, and slew all the male children that were in Bethlehem, and in all the coasts thereof, from two years old and under, according to the time which he had diligently enquired of the wise men.

Every time I read about the babies being killed and slaughtered, it always really bothered me. I remember lying in bed many nights thinking that these babies must have been given something special for having to die in place of Jesus, which I thought at the time was His birth-given name, from my Christian upbringing. Later, I learned it was not but Immanuel. That is when I started studying this topic. Through my studies, I realized that He did do something special for them, and this study is the proof.

Matt. 2:17-18

17 Then was fulfilled that which was spoken by Jeremiah the prophet saying,

[18] In Rama there was a voice heard, lamentation, and weeping, and great mourning, Rachel weeping for her children, and would not be comforted, because they are not.

PROPHESIED IN JEREMIAH 31:15.

Rachel was the wife of Jacob. From his twelve sons came the twelve tribes of Israel. These babies were foreordained for their lives to be taken for the fulfillment of this prophecy, just as John the Baptist was foreordained in his mother's womb.

They would be the first fruits of the Messiah. Now that we know these male babies were the first fruits, and the Messiah cannot be called the first fruits since He is only one, this makes Him the first fruit of those who slept. We can now understand how the following scripture should be read.

YES, only those 144,000 babies.

REVELATION CHAPTER 14

[1] And I looked, and, lo, a Lamb stood on the mount Zion, and with him a hundred forty *and* four thousand, having his Father's name written on their foreheads.

2 And I heard a voice from heaven, as the voice of many waters, and as the voice of a great thunder: and I heard the voice of harpers harping with their harps:

3 And they sung as it were a new song before the throne, and before the four beasts, and the elders: and no man could learn that song but the hundred *and* forty *and* four thousand, which were redeemed from the earth.

4 These are they which were not defiled with women; for they are virgins. These are they which follow the Lamb whithersoever he goeth. These were redeemed from among men, *being* the first fruits unto Yahweh and to the Lamb.

5 And in their mouth was found no guile: for they are without fault before the throne of Yahweh.

THE BABIES were killed. Then Immanuel was hung on an Olive tree with rope from his wrists and resurrected. Babies went to heaven with Immanuel, but not as babies. They follow him wherever he goes and are with him now.

1 Cor. 15:20-23

20 But now is the Messiah risen from the dead, and become the firstfruits of them that slept. 21: For since by man came death, by man came also the resurrection of the dead.

22 For as in Adam all die, even so in the Messiah shall all be made alive.

23 But every man in his own order: the Messiah the firstfruits, afterward they that are the Messiah's at his coming.

The following is the corrected version of the above scripture. The corrections are in ( ):

1 Cor. 15:20-23

20 But now is the Messiah risen from the dead and become the firstfruit of them that slept.

21 For since by man came death, by man came also the resurrection of the dead.

22 For as in Adam all die, even so in the Messiah shall all be made alive.

23 But every man in his own order: the Messiah (,) the first Fruits, afterward they that are the Messiah's at his coming.

Notice there is a comma between the Messiah and the first Fruits in verse 23 above.

Thirty-some years after these babies were murdered and buried, they appeared to their parents, families, and witnesses. Those who had witnessed their murders and burials also witnessed their resurrection. All these events took place within these people's lifetimes, so there could be no greater witnesses to these babies' resurrection. When reading the scriptures, you will find that Yahweh always has a witness for whatever He does.

2 Timothy 2:18 Who concerning the truth have erred, saying that the resurrection is past already; and overthrow the faith of some.

It seems that some people who knew about the resurrection of these babies went around telling others that the resurrection had already taken place. As a result, some people believed that the resurrection had already occurred.

I must prove one more thing before going on to the second 144,000 in Ch. 7 of Revelation.

The killing of these babies may have started in Bethlehem, but it spread over all of Judaea because Joseph was told to go back to Judaea from Egypt after the death of Herod. Once he got there, he heard Herod's son was reigning over Judaea and he was afraid to go there. Yahweh even warned him in a dream not to go. So, the murder still had to be going on at this time.

Matt. 2:19-23

19 But when Herod was dead, behold, a Messenger of Yahweh appeareth in a dream to Joseph in Egypt.

20 Saying, Arise, and take the young child and his mother, and go into the land of Judaea: for they are dead which sought the young child's life.

21 And he arose, and took the young child and his mother, and came into the land of Zion.

22 But when he heard that Archelaus did reign in Judaea in the room of his father Herod, he was afraid to go thither: notwithstanding, being warned of Yahweh in a dream, he turned aside into the parts of Galilee:

113

²³ And he came and dwelt in a city called Nazareth: that it might be fulfilled which was spoken by the prophets, He shall be called a Nazarene.

CHAPTER 15
WHAT THEY DID; FULFILLED THE ABOVE CHAPTER 14 PROPHECY. THEY WERE NOT KINGS SINCE THEY WERE CALLED WISE MEN AND WENT BEFORE KING HEROD

NOW TO PROVE WHAT THE STAR WAS:

Matthew 2:1

1 Now when Immanuel was born in Bethlehem of Judah/ Galilee in the days of Herod the king, behold, there came wise men from the east to Zion,

2 Saying, Where is he that is born King of the Jews: for we have seen his star in the east, and are come to worship him.

THEY WERE JEWS NOT GENTILES.

Notice here they saw the star. The star did not lead them to Bethlehem, where Immanuel was born, but to Zion.

7 Then Herod, when he had privately called the wise men, inquired of them diligently what time the star appeared.

Notice the star did not exist until it appeared.

Matthew 2:9-10. When they had heard the king, they departed; and, lo, the star, which they saw in the east, WENT BEFORE THEM. Till IT CAME and STOOD OVER where the young child was.

Notice here that the star, when they departed, appeared to them again and went before them and took them to the very house Immanuel was living in.

[10] When they saw the star, they rejoiced with exceeding great joy.

Why were they exceedingly joyous when they saw the star? THEY SEEN WHAT IT ACTUALLY WAS.

This was a spacecraft, not a star. A star can lead you in a direction; it cannot move, so you can follow it, and it cannot take you to a specific location. It was not until they came to the house and saw what they thought looked like a star was a spacecraft and that they were joyous when they saw it.

CHAPTER 16
HOW THE MESSIAH FULFILLED THE FEASTS

SPRING FEASTS:

Feast of Passover - Became the offered Lamb.

Feast of Unleavened Bread - Was buried - last supper, "This is my body."

7th Day Sabbath - He was resurrected.

Feast of First Fruits - He was the priest who offered unto the Father the First Fruits of his wave offering of the 144,000 babies, the first fruits.

Feast of Pentecost - 50 days after the Feast of First Fruits came to Pentecost, which was fulfilled with the outpouring of His Spirit.

The 3 Feasts that are not fulfilled yet will be fulfilled upon His return.

FALL FEASTS:

Yom Teruah - Feast of Trumpets - Leviticus 23:23-25

23 And Yahweh spake unto Moses, saying,

24 Speak unto the children of Judaea, saying, In the seventh month, in the first day of the month, shall ye have a Sabbath, a memorial of blowing of trumpets, an righteous convocation.

25 Ye shall do no servile work therein: but ye shall offer an offering made by fire unto Yahweh. Feast of Trumpets starts on a full moon.

Matthew 24:29-31

29 Immediately after the tribulation of those days shall the sun be darkened, and the moon shall not give her light, and the stars shall fall from heaven, and the powers of the heavens shall be shaken:

30 And then shall appear the sign of the Son of man in heaven: and then shall all the tribes of the earth mourn, and they shall see the Son of man coming in the clouds of heaven with power and great honor.

31 And he shall send his Messengers with a great sound of a trumpet, and they shall gather together his elect from the four winds, from one end of heaven to the other.

1 Corinthians 15:51-52

51 Behold, I shew you a mystery; We shall not all sleep, but we shall all be changed,

52 In a moment, in the twinkling of an eye, at the last trump: for the trumpet shall sound, and the dead shall be raised incorruptible, and we shall be changed.

1 Thessalonians 3:16 For Yahweh Himself shall descend from heaven with a shout, with the voice of the arch- messenger, and with the trump of Yahweh: and the dead in Yahweh shall rise first:

SEE HOW HE COULD NOT HAVE BEEN BORN DURING THE FEAST OF TRUMPETS?

YOM KIPPUR - FEAST OF ATONEMENT / JUDGMENT - NOAH AND THE COMING BACK OF YAHWEH COMPARED.

A. Noah warned 7 days before the flood came:

Genesis 7:4 For yet seven days, and I will cause it to rain upon the earth forty days and forty nights; and every living substance that I have made will I destroy from off the face of the earth.

B. People are warned 7 Years before Yahweh returns; 7-Year Peace Treaty:

Daniel 9:27 And he shall confirm the covenant with many for one week: and in the midst of the week he shall cause the offerings to cease, and for the overspreading of abominations he shall make it desolate, even until the consummation, and that determined shall be poured upon the desolate.

C. Noah takes all those who are going to be saved from the flood onto the Ark:

Genesis 7:13 In the selfsame day entered Noah, and Shem, and Ham, and Japheth, the sons of Noah, and Noah's wife, and the three wives of his sons with them, into the ark.

D. Yahweh takes all those who are going to be saved into the spacecraft:

1 Thessalonians 4:16-17

16 For Yahweh Himself shall descend from heaven with a shout, with the voice of the arch-messenger, and with the trump of Yahweh: and the dead in Yahweh Messiah shall rise first

[17] Then we which are alive and remain shall be (caught up together with them in the clouds,) to meet Yahweh in the air; and so shall we ever be with Yahweh.

E. Noah's Ark raised them up above the wicked that were killed:

Genesis 7:18 And the waters prevailed, and were increased greatly upon the earth; and the ark went upon the face of the waters.

The wicked were killed off.

F. Yahweh's spacecraft raises His Elect above those who were killed.

Luke 16:26 "And beside all this, between us and you there is a great gulf fixed: so that they which would pass from hence to you cannot; neither can they pass to us, that would come from thence."

The wicked were killed off.

G. Noah's Ark came down on Mount Ararat:

Genesis 8:4 And the ark rested in the seventh month, on the seventeenth day of the month, upon the mountains of Ararat.

H. Yahweh's spacecraft comes down on Mount of Olives:

Zechariah 14:4 And his feet shall stand in that day upon the mount of Olives, which is before Zion on the east, and the mount of Olives shall cleave in the midst thereof toward the east and toward the west, and there shall be a very great valley; and half of the mountain shall remove toward the north, and half of it toward the south.

I. Noah's family re-populates the earth:

Genesis 9:1 And Yahweh blessed Noah and his sons, and said unto them, Be fruitful, and multiply, and replenish the earth.

J. Those who never heard the truth re-populate the earth:

Isaiah 35:10 And the ransomed of Yahweh shall return and come to Zion with songs and everlasting joy upon their heads: they shall obtain joy and gladness, and sorrow and sighing shall flee away.

Daniel 7:12 As concerning the rest of the beasts, they had their dominion taken away: (yet their lives were prolonged for a season and time.)

Jeremiah 16:19 "O Yahweh, my strength, and my fortress, and my refuge in the day of affliction, the Gentiles shall come unto thee from the ends of the earth, and shall say, surely our fathers have inherited lies, vanity, and things wherein there is no profit."

Jeremiah 3:17 At that time they will call Zion the throne of Yahweh and all nations will gather in Zion to honor the name of Yahweh. No longer will they follow the stubbornness of their evil hearts.

Revelation 22:14-15

14 Blessed are they that do his commandments, that they may have right to the tree of life and may enter in through the gates into the city.

15 For without are dogs, and sorcerers, and whoremongers, and murderers, and idolaters, and whosoever loveth and maketh a lie.

NOTE: Why are all those in verse 15 above without and unable to enter the gates of the city? Because these are those who had never heard the whole truth and were raised from the dead after Yahweh's return to be taught by Yahweh Himself the whole truth. This way, there will be no excuses if they are deceived by Satan when he deceives the world one last time before the White Throne Judgment. They will have the choice to serve either Satan or Yahweh. Those who choose Yahweh will be filled with His Spirit, which gives salvation, while those who serve Satan will be thrown into the Lake of Fire and never exist again.

SUKKOT - FEAST OF TABERNACLES - HE WILL COMPLETELY FULFILL THE FEAST OF TABERNACLES WHEN HE GATHERS THE HARVEST OF THE ELECT FOR THE MILLENNIAL KINGDOM.

John 1:14 And the Word became flesh and pitched His tent among us, and we saw His honor, honor as of an only brought-forth of a father, complete in favor and truth.

Hebrews 9:11 But Messiah being come a high priest of good things to come, by a greater and more perfect tabernacle, not made with hands, that is to say, not of this building."

"When you ride the train of Christianity, you ride the tracks of paganism." By Gary W. Stanfield

CHAPTER 17
HOW CHRISTIANITY STARTED ITS BELIEF SYSTEM THROUGH THE YEARS, STARTING OUT WITH WHAT WAS ADDED BY CONSTANTINE AND THEN OTHERS

The beginnings of the belief system started by Constantine were continually added to over the years, culminating in the formation of the Catholic denomination. This new denomination incorporated many old beliefs and remained true to the added pagan beliefs from that time forward. Our ancestors who lived through those times as Christians believed these teachings, which perpetuated through the centuries up to today.

In 340 C.E., December 25 (the rebirth or birthday of all sun deities) was established as the birth of Jesus. They merged these two sun deities into one, but there are three: Ea-Zeus = "Jesus" = Ea-ZEUS. EA IS THE GREEK DEITY OF HEALING, the Healing Zeus. Now, why would Yahweh name His son after Zeus? He would not. Research reveals that the name "Jesus" is linked to the Greek deity "Zeus."

According to "COME OUT OF HER MY PEOPLE" by C. J. Koster, "Jesus" was a name given to Him after His death by Constantine and his pagan bishops. Constantine was the one who started the office of Bishop.

Mosaic of Jesus as *Christo Sole* (Christ the Sun) in Mausoleum M in the pre-fourth-century necropolis under St. Peter's Basilica St Peter's in Rome

It is sometimes forgotten that the early Christians associated Jesus with the Sun. Among the church fathers, Cyprian speaks of Christ as Sol Verus, the "True Sun."

All the so-called church fathers were pagans.

Jesus' birth is December 25 (Christmas), the rebirth or birthday of all sun deities.

WHY? Because it is the birthday of Nimrod and all the sun deity names are from many different cultures that worshiped Nimrod in many different names.

Christianity imported the Saturnalia festival, hoping to take the pagan masses in with it. Christian leaders succeeded in converting to Christianity large numbers of pagans by promising them that they could continue to celebrate the Saturnalia as Christians. All that was left after the persecutions were the pagans.

In the fourth century, the Roman Emperor Constantine united all pagan religious factions under one composite deity: Hesus = Ea-Zeus.

Ea was the Greek deity of healing, and Zeus was a sun deity. Additionally, Krishna (or Christos, Christ) was another pagan sun deity. Thus, three pagan deities were compounded to make one. This amalgamation created the practice of the pagan Babylonian Mystery Religion under the name of Christianity, designed to absorb all pagan belief systems. Christianity, as it is known today, originated in Rome, not Zion, and is the modern-day name for the old Babylonian religious system started by Nimrod.

The Pontifex Maximus is a title for the leaders of the Babylonian Mystery Cult, traced back to Babylon with Nimrod as the first Pontifex Maximus. This is why the Pope is said to sit on Satan/Nimrod's Throne. Therefore, when the Papacy claims that they can trace their line back to Simon Peter as the first Pope, it is a falsehood.

Pagan Rome turned into Papal Rome with only one religion allowed, and it began with the CROSS!! A sun symbol.

313 C.E., Constantine introduced the Babylonian mystery religions into one as a Christian religion, and *he made Christianity*

The Edict of Milan, issued by Constantine, established Christianity as the official state religion of the Roman Empire. Constantine incorporated pagan elements and followers into the newly constituted Roman Empire to unify his subjects under a single religious framework.

317 C.E., First Constantine coin with a Cross.

320 C.E., The lighting of candles

341 C.E., Constantius II (Flavius Julius Constantius) persecutes "all the soothsayers and the Hellenists." Many gentile Hellenes are either imprisoned or executed.

In 325 C.E., the Council of Nicea discussed a 40-day Lenten season of fasting. Until the 600s, Lent began on Quadragesima (Fortieth) Sunday, but Gregory the Great (c. 540-604) moved it to a Wednesday, now called Ash Wednesday. In the fifth century, St. Augustine declared that all unbaptized babies went to hell upon death. By the Middle Ages, this idea was softened to suggest a less severe fate known as limbo.

359 C.E., In Skythopolis, Syria, the Christians organize the first death camps for the torture and executions of the arrested non-Christians from all around the empire.

364 C.E., Emperor Jovian orders the burning of the Library of Antioch. An Imperial edict (11th September) orders the death penalty for all those who worship their ancestral deities or practice divination. Three different edicts (4th February, 9th September, and 23rd December) order the confiscation of all properties of the pagan temples and the death penalty for participation in pagan rituals, even private ones.

They made the pagan temples Christian churches.

364 C.E. decreed, "Christians shall not Judaize and be idle on Saturday but shall work on that day; but the Lord's Day they shall especially honor, and, as being Christians, shall, if possible, do no work on that day. If, however, they are found Judaizing, they shall be shut out from Christ" (Strand, op. cit., citing Charles J. Hefele, A History of the Councils of the Church, 2 [Edinburgh, 1876] 316).

370 C.E., Valens orders a tremendous persecution of non-Christian peoples in all the Eastern Empire. In Antioch, among many other non-Christians, the ex-governor Fidustius and the priests Hilarius and Patricius are executed. The philosopher Simonides is burned alive, and the philosopher Maximus is decapitated. Tons of books are burnt in the squares of the cities of the Eastern Empire.

372 C.E., Valens orders the governor of Minor Asia to exterminate all the Hellenes and all documents of their wisdom.

373 C.E., The term "pagan" (Pagani, villagers, equivalent to the modern insult, "peasants") is introduced by the Christians to demean non-believers. The non-Christians are called "loathsome, heretics, stupid, and blind." In another edict, Theodosius calls "insane" those who do not believe in the Christian God. The Christian priests lead the angry mob against the temple of goddess Demeter in Eleusis and try to lynch the hierophants Nestorius and Priskus.

375 C.E., The worship of saints.

The highest office in the pagan pantheon was that of Pontifex Maximus or Supreme Pontiff... This was held by the Roman Caesars. Constantine was the last Caesar/Pontifex Maximus of the Roman Empire. Constantine, during the time of being the head of Christianity, had not only his eldest son killed but also his wife.

Constantine was a sun worshipper who mixed sun worship with Judaism to form the pagan religion of Christianity, the apostate religion that Scriptures speak of—one that looks like the truth but is not, and that would deceive even the very elect if possible. Pagans were baptized but continued their pagan ways with a different meaning and under a new name. For instance, if pagans worshipped a tree, the priests would consecrate it in the name of Jesus Christ and let them continue their worship. This is similar to what happened with the Egyptian Pharaohs, where the High Priest became as powerful as the Pharaoh. Eventually, the High Priest took over the power of the Pharaoh, and the displaced Pharaoh moved to another area, assuming the title of High Priest as well. They, too, had a system where the secular had authority over the religious and the religious over the secular.

"...the appellation of G/d had been confirmed by Constantine on the Pope, who being G/d, cannot be judged by man." Pope Nicholas I, quoted in History of the Councils, bol.IX, Dist.: 96 Can 7, "Satis Evidentur Decret Gratian Primer Para," by Labbe and Cossart.

History teaches that the Roman Empire ended in the 400s and that the Holy Roman Empire started in 800 when Charlemagne was crowned Emperor by Pope Leo III. But what really happened in that 400-year gap between these two so-called empires? This period is often unclear, but one plausible explanation is that Constantine was the first Pontifex Maximus (Pope) over Christianity, making it the state religion of the Roman Empire. This would make Constantine both the last Emperor of the Roman Empire and the first Pope of Christianity. Under this scenario, the Roman Empire continued with a new title for its leaders.

The Germans started calling the Roman Empire the Holy Roman Empire with Otto I's coronation in 962. However, scriptures state that the Roman Empire would be the last, which fits Constantine's scenario. At the Battle of Milvian Bridge, Constantine saw a cross and was told, "IN THIS SIGN CONQUER." According to "Life of Constantine" by Eusebius, Constantine had a cross put on the shields of his soldiers, and his soldiers, when they marched, were to be preceded only by the standard of the cross, not by the Roman golden eagles.

The cross is the mark of this Religious Babylonian Government Beast/Papacy, which Yahweh Messiah will destroy upon His return. The Caesars or Emperors held the title Pontifex Maximus since they were over both secular and religious government and the head of the Roman Empire, which encompassed all of humanity at that time. Thus, they held the title of Pope.

When Constantine started Christianity and the Papacy, he changed the Roman Government from being secular over religious to religious over secular. He also changed his title from Emperor to Pope Constantine. The Catholic denomination of Christianity, which started in 1559 during the Council of Trent, produced a list of Popes that supposedly goes back to Peter. However, Peter was never part of any of this, and the church leaders know it. The Pontifex Maximus title traces back to the first person holding that title, Nimrod, who turned his back on Yahweh and started paganism, becoming the first to establish a kingdom on earth.

The cross is also a sun symbol for pagan sun worshipers like Constantine. This mark of the Religious Babylonian Government Beast/Papacy will be destroyed by Yahweh Messiah upon His return.

381 C.E., On 2nd May, Theodosius deprived all Christians of their rights who returned to the pagan religion. At the Council of Constantinople, the 'Holy Spirit' (There is no such thing called a Holy Spirit.) is declared 'Divine' (thus sanctioning a triune deity). Throughout the Eastern Empire, the pagan temples and libraries were looted or burned down.

ROME AND JEROME'S LATIN VULGATE:

382 C.E., Jerome was commissioned by Bishop Damasus to *revise* the popular Latin translation of the Vulgate.

Jerome collected Constantine's manuscripts compiling the Latin Vulgate, which became the only scriptures available for the next 1000 years that Jerome completed in 405 C.E.

2 Peter 2:1 But there were false prophets also among the people, even as there shall be false teachers among you, who privily shall bring in damnable heresies, even denying Yahweh that bought them, and bring upon themselves swift destruction.

I believe the Vatican is sitting on the genuine original manuscripts with the true name of the Messiah up to this day. They still have

Constantine's books that were made from the Word of Yahweh written in Hebrew, and Constantine transferred them to Greek.

385 to 388 C.E., Thousands of innocent pagans from all sides of the empire suffered martyrdom in the notorious death camps of Skythopolis.

In 389 to 390 C.E., hordes of fanatic Christian hermits from the desert flooded the cities of the Middle East and Egypt. They destroyed statues, altars, libraries, and pagan temples and lynched pagans. Theophilus, Patriarch of Alexandria, initiated heavy persecutions against non-Christian peoples, converting the temple of Dionysius into a Christian church, burning down the Mithraeum of the city, and destroying the temple of Zeus. He also mocked the pagan priests before they were killed by stoning. The Christian mob profaned the cult images.

391 C.E., The Great Library of Alexandria in Egypt was burned.

392 C.E., On 8th November, Theodosius outlaws all non-Christian rituals and names them "superstitions of the gentiles" (gentilicia superstitio). New full-scale persecutions were ordered against pagans. The Mysteries of Samothrace were ended, and the priests slaughtered. In Cyprus, the local bishops "Saint" Epiphanius and "Saint" Tychon destroyed all the temples of the island and exterminated thousands of non-Christians.

394 C.E., The mass was adopted - The Mass, according to the Catechism of the Roman Universal Church, duplicates the sacrifice on the cross. Quoting directly, "The Mass is the same sacrifice as the sacrifice on the cross, because in the Mass the victim is the same, and the principal Priest is the same, Jesus Christ." [My Catholic Faith, p. 286] The term "sacrifice" comes from the concept of something being made sacred. The cross is also a symbol used in pagan sun worship, representing a sun symbol.

Mass is a ceremony that, in Christian pagan terminology, sacrifices Jesus Christ repeatedly, that is repeated daily all over the world, while they are being deceived into thinking they are honoring the Messiah for what he had done.

Mythology's Last Gods - p. 237 -238: It was this combination of the consonants of Yahweh and the vowels of Adonai, transcribed into German, that gave rise to the mongrel word Jehovah, used by no Jews and only unlearned Christians. When the Christian masochist Jerome translated the Jewish scriptures into Latin around 400 C.E., he was sufficiently intimidated by the Jewish taboo to change Yahweh to Dominus, Latin for Adonai, and this, in turn, led to the eventual production of English bibles in which Yahweh was never mentioned but was replaced by a character called "the Lord." The scriptures were locked up and hidden in the Latin tongue. Only priests, such as Wycliffe, Tyndale, and Luther, were allowed to teach the scriptures, and only in Latin. By the time these men began the Reformation, the lie had already been in existence for nearly a thousand years. Lord and Adonai are sun deity names.

At the time, Latin was used only in governmental and religious proceedings. Latin was not understood by the common and the uneducated. The only thing Wycliff, Tyndale, and Luther had to work with to start their individual translation of the scriptures was the Latin Vulgate. They shared the Vulgate, which is said that it was corrupt and inaccurate, as the only source text. In the 1400s, the Latin Vulgate was the first book printed from type.

395 C.E., Two new edicts (22nd July and 7th August) cause new persecutions against pagans. Rufinus, the eunuch Prime Minister of Emperor Flavius Arcadius, directed the hordes of baptized Goths (led by Alaric) to the country of the Hellenes. Encouraged by Christian monks, the barbarians sack and burn many cities (Dion, Delphi, Megara, Corinth, Pheneos, Argos, Nemea, Lycosoura, Sparta, Messene, Phigaleia, Olympia, etc.), slaughtered or enslaved

innumerable gentile Hellenes and burned down all the temples. Among others, they burned down the Eleusinian Sanctuary and burned alive all its priests (including the hierophant of Mithras Hilariu).

ROME AND THE CHRISTIANS HAD TO KILL OFF ALL THE PAGANS WHO WOULD NOT COME OVER TO CHRISTIANITY SINCE IT WAS THE UNIVERSAL RELIGION OF THE ROMAN EMPIRE, WITH NO OTHER RELIGION BEING ALLOWED.

399 C.E., With a new edict (13th July), Flavius Arcadius orders all remaining pagan temples, mainly in the countryside, to be immediately demolished.

400 C.E., The word "Bible" was first used.

405 C.E., Jerome's Latin Vulgate, the only scripture available for over 1000 years, was locked up in the Latin tongue.

401 C.E., The Christian mob of Carthage lynches non-Christians and destroys temples and "idols." In Gaza, too, the local bishop "Saint" Porphyrius sends his followers to lynch pagans and demolish the remaining nine still-active temples of the city.

In the fifth century, St. Augustine declared that all unbaptized babies went to hell upon death. By the Middle Ages, the idea was softened to suggest a less severe fate, limbo.

405 C.E., John Chrysostom sends hordes of grey-dressed monks armed with clubs and iron bars to destroy the "idols" in all the cities of Palestine.

408 C.E., Local bishops lead new heavy persecutions against pagans and new book burning. Judges who show pity for the pagans are also persecuted. "Saint" Augustine massacres hundreds of protesting pagans in Calama, Algeria.

409 C.E., Another edict orders all methods of divination, including astrology, to be punished by death.

415 C.E., In Alexandria, the Christian mob, urged by Bishop Cyril, attacks a few days before the Judeo-Christian Pascha (Easter) and cuts to pieces the famous and beautiful philosopher Hypatia. The pieces of her body, carried around by the Christian mob through the streets of Alexandria, are finally burned together with her books in a place called Cynaron.

416 C.E., The inquisitor Hypatius, alias "The Sword of God," exterminates the last pagans of Bithynia. In Constantinople (7th December), all non-Christian army officers, public employees, and judges are dismissed.

423 C.E., Emperor Theodosius II declares (8th June) that the religion of the pagans is nothing more than "demon worship" and orders all those who persist in practicing it to be punished by imprisonment and torture.

431 C.E., The title "Mother of God" was officially conferred upon Mary at the Council of Ephesus.

432 C.E., The worship of Mary began to develop.

435 C.E., On 14th November, a new edict by Theodosius II orders the death penalty for all "heretics" and pagans of the empire. Only Judaism is considered a legal non-Christian religion.

448 C.E., Theodosius II orders all non-Christian books to be burned.

450 C.E., All the temples of Aphrodisias (the city of the female deity Aphrodite) are demolished, and all its libraries are burned down. The city is renamed Stavroupolis (City of the Cross).

482 to 488 C.E., The majority of the pagans of Minor Asia are exterminated after a desperate revolt against the emperor and the Church.

500 C.E., Priests began to assume distinctive robes.

515 C.E., The Emperor of Constantinople, Anastasius, orders the massacre of the pagans in the Arabian city Zoara and the demolition of the temple of the local god Theandrites.

526 C.E., Extreme Unction

546 C.E., Hundreds of pagans are put to death in Constantinople by the inquisitor Ioannis Asiacus.

556 C.E., Justinian orders the notorious inquisitor Amantius to go to Antioch to find, arrest, torture, and exterminate the last non-Christians of the city and burn all the private libraries down.

From 578 to 582 C.E., Christians tortured and crucified Hellenes all around the Eastern Empire and exterminated the last non-Christians of Heliopolis (Baalbek).

591 C.E., The Crucifix was made the symbol of Christianity.

591 C.E., Islam was started. In fact, Islam was initiated. Islam was started by the Papacy, and that is why they have so much in common.

593 C.E., The doctrine of purgatory was introduced.

600 C.E., Worship in Latin (since repealed) was mandated. Also, prayers to the dead.

606 C.E., Claims to Papal Supremacy took firm foot.

633 C.E., The Council of Toledo made a strict rule that all priests must receive the circular tonsure on the crown of the head. This had to do with sun and moon worship in honor of the solar disc.

650 C.E., Feasts in honor of the Virgin Mary.

709 C.E., The custom of kissing the Pope's foot was introduced.

750 C.E., Pope speaks for Yahweh Himself.

772 - 804 C.E., Saxon Wars - against the Saxons, a confederation of Germanic tribes, the objective of these campaigns was to Christianize the pagans, as these people were then considered, and to expand the borders of the Frankish kingdom under Charlemagne. The Saxon Wars ended in 804. Altogether, eighteen battles were fought and resulted in the incorporation of Saxony into the Frankish realm and their conversion from Germanic paganism to Germanic Christianity.

787 C.E., The worship of images and relics was authorized. Images were placed in the churches, and the people were encouraged to bow down and pray to them. They were first commanded to do so by the Second Council of Nicea. A.D. 787 - Barontus, Ecclesiastical Annals, Vol. 9, pp. 391-404, Antwerp. 1612; Charles J. Hefele, History of the Councils of the Church from the Original Documents, BK 18, chap. 1, secs. 332-333, COPYRIGHT 1994.

850 C.E., The invention of holy water.

Nicholas I (858–67):

'It is evident that the Popes can neither be bound nor unbound by any earthly power, nor even by that of the apostle [Peter] if he should return upon the earth; since Constantine the Great has recognized that the pontiffs held the place of G/d upon earth, the divinity not being able to be judged by any living man. We are, then, infallible, and whatever may be our acts, we are not accountable for them but to ourselves' (A Woman Rides the Beast, Dave Hunt, pp. 153–154, copyright 1994.)

Scriptures speak of only the Roman Empire as being the last empire. Constantine started Christianity and was the one who changed the Roman Empire from a secular over the religious government to a religious over the secular government by making Christianity the state religion of the Roman Empire and having anyone who did not convert. Constantine wanted all pagan religions under one heading, which started what is known today as the Papacy. The Roman Empire never changed its name; we still live in the Roman Empire era today. Scriptures do not speak of another empire after the Roman Empire; it will be the last until Yahweh starts His kingdom here on earth. The great falling away took place during the 11 Persecutions of the Emperors of the Roman Empire, and this was also when all the true believers in Yahweh Messiah were killed off. It was Constantine who revealed who the Anti-Messiah and Man of Transgressions was, none other than the Pontifex Maximus, which is traced back to Nimrod, the very first false messiah who started paganism and turned his back on Yahweh. Constantine became the first Pope/Emperor of the Roman Empire. This Babylonian Religious Government System is what Yahweh will destroy at His coming, which was started by Nimrod. Known today as the Papacy, it will rise back up through the 10 Kings who have no kingdom yet but will give their power to the Pope. These 10 Kings come from the 10 World Unions being put together today.

Napoleon took the Pope's power away; now, the deadly wound is being healed as we watch the Pope regaining his power. There was never anything called the Holy Roman Empire until 962 C.E., when the Holy Roman Empire officially began - a political entity in Europe that began with the papal coronation of Otto I. So, it was the emperors who killed the believers back then, and it will be the Pope who would kill the last-day believers in Yahweh Messiah. The Pope is the only personage that fits all the prophecies about the Anti-Messiah and False Prophet, Man of Transgressions, and the Image of the Beast. The Little Horn Constantine (Pontifex Maximus/Pope) of Daniel has been followed throughout history since Constantine as it deceives the world with its smokescreens to cover up the truth.

What people must understand is that Constantine did not change the faith of Yahweh and His truths, which he could never have done. But what he did do was start a pagan religion with an already existing one by the same name of Christianity to put all the pagans under one heading and use the Word of Yahweh that he had propagandized to deceive people to believe in his pagan lies and his pagan Christianity. People believe that Constantine changed Yahweh's Sabbath; no, what he did was make Sunday the Sabbath for his pagan religion, Christianity. The pagans were used to worshiping the Sun on Sunday, so he stayed true to his pagan belief system even though it looked like he had changed Yahweh's Sabbath, which he could never have done. This is how Satan's deceit works.

So, Constantine started all of this when the world fully became Satan's. As you will be able to see, it is going to end the same way it was started, with the Pope and Christianity, when Yahweh ends it all.

890 C.E., Worship of St. Joseph.

927 C.E., College of Cardinals established.

965 C.E., the Baptism of Bells started.

993 C.E., The canonization of saints was formalized.

998 C.E., Fasting on Fridays and during Lent begins.

1003 C.E., Feasts for the Dead were introduced.

1050 C.E., The blasphemous Catholic Mass, which is a sacrifice.

1054, The Great Schism - Christian versus Christian

In the Eastern and Western branches of Christendom, the Eastern Patriarch rejected the demands and excommunicated the Pope from the Church for rejecting his supremacy, and the Pope returned the favor. While they were both Christian, they were rivals. Constantinople, the capital of Byzantium, was the head of the Eastern Christian Church, just like Rome was the head of the Western Christian Church.

1074 C.E., The celibacy of the priesthood was declared.

1076 C.E., The dogma of Papal infallibility was announced.

1090 C.E., Rosary Prayer Beads were introduced.

1095 C.E., Pope Urban II remitted all penance of persons who participated in the crusades, the first known plenary indulgences.

1140 C.E., The doctrine that there are seven sacraments was introduced.

1170 and 1200 C.E., Purgatory as a physical place rather than merely as a state.

1184 C.E., the Inquisition in operation for centuries, now made official by the Council of Verona.

1190 C.E., The sale of indulgences.

1200 C.E., The wafer was substituted for the loaf.

The Church began claiming that it had a "treasury" of indulgences (consisting of the merits of Christ and the saints) that it could dispense in ways that promoted the Church and its mission.

1215 C.E., The dogma of transubstantiation was adopted.

Confession was instituted. Confession of transgressions to a priest

1220 C.E., The adoration of the Wafer.

1229 C.E., the Council of Valencia puts Scriptures on the forbidden list.

1251 C.E., Protection by a piece of cloth (scapular).

1274 C.E., PURGATORY of Catholic doctrine. At the Second Council of Lyon, the Christian, not Catholic Church, defined, for the first time, its teaching on purgatory in two points: some souls are purified after death; such souls benefit from the prayers and pious duties that the living do for them.

The idea of purgatory has roots that date back to antiquity. A sort of proto-purgatory called the "celestial Hades" appears in the writings of Plato and Heraclides Pontius, and in many other pagan writers. This concept is distinguished from the Hades of the underworld described in the works of Homer and Hesiod.

According to the French historian Jacques Le Goff, the conception of purgatory as a physical place dates to the 12th century, the heyday of medieval otherworld-journey narratives and of pilgrims' tales about St. Patrick's Purgatory, a cave-like entrance to purgatory on a remote island in Northern Ireland.

1300 C.E. "Limbo of Infants."

1316 C.E., The Ave Maria was introduced.

1300s's LIMBO: From the Latin "limbus," for hem or edge, limbo refers to a "state of natural happiness" outside heaven, a destination for the souls of babies who were not baptized and certain virtuous people, such as faithful Jews who lived before the time of Christ. Limbo, which comes from the Latin word meaning "border" or "edge," was considered by medieval theologians to be a state or place reserved for the unbaptized dead, including good people who lived before the coming of Christ. In the fifth century, St. Augustine declared that all unbaptized babies went to hell upon death. By the Middle Ages, the idea was softened to suggest a less severe fate: limbo. Never part of formal doctrine because it does not appear in Scripture, limbo was removed from the Catholic Catechism in 1992.

Early in the 14th century, "SCRIPTURES" took the place of using the word "BIBLE" in Christianity. The word in Middle English also could mean "a writing, an act of writing, written characters" (mid-14th c.), a sense now rare. The sense of is by late 14th c. Figuratively, something assuredly true was attested by the 1570s as an adjective, "relating to the Scriptures," by 1720.

1343 C.E., Pope Clement VI declared, "The merits of Christ are a treasure of indulgences."

1380's, Wycliffe's New Testament. - English. The corrupt readings in Jerome's Latin Vulgate found their way into the English, French, Spanish, and Italian Versions. This was the only scripture that Wycliffe, Tyndale, and Luther had to start theirs with, and then they had each other's. Wycliffe argued that the Scriptures did little good locked away in Latin that few could understand. God's Word, he declared, is for all people: 'No man is so rude a scholar but that he might learn the words of the Gospel according to his simplicity.' Wycliffe thus determined to give the English people a translation that could be read in their native tongue. He and his associates completed the monumental task in about 1382. Wycliffe's translation was based on the Latin Vulgate, as he and his colleagues knew no Hebrew or Greek.

1415 C.E., The cup was taken from the laity.

1439 C.E., Purgatory was officially decreed.

1508 C.E., the First part of the "Ave Maria" saying is made official.

1516 C.E., Erasmus's New Testament. - Greek. Erasmus took monastic vows and was a lifelong, devoted son of the Roman Church. No one put the Greek New Testament in print until 1516. The churchmen and scholars had the authoritative Vulgate, so what need was there, they thought, to have Greek? Erasmus translated Jerome's Latin Vulgate into Greek, which is what Constantine had his pagan translation done in Greek from the original Hebrew.

The Textus Receptus, or "received text," refers to the first published Greek New Testament edited by Desiderius Erasmus in 1516 and later, with some changes, by Stephanus, Beza, and Elzivir. This text was initially compiled using only seven late Greek manuscripts (11th-13th centuries). The Textus Receptus became the underlying text for many important translations, including the King James Version. (SEE UNDER 1624 C.E.).

Since the Latin Vulgate was the only scripture for over 1000 years, the only place these other Greek manuscripts could have come from was the Vatican itself.

The work on the Greek text was hastily and carelessly done. Erasmus' biographer Froude characterized him: "haste made him careless, and this fault always clung to him" (p. 8). Erasmus himself admitted that the work on his first edition "was done too hastily" (Froude, p. 189). He declared that the work was more precipitated than edited. Though Erasmus had spent fifteen years editing the works of Jerome and ten years preparing a new Latin translation of the New Testament, he spent less than ten months, or rather part of ten months, in editing the Greek New Testament. The printer's work showed the haste in the production as the book had numerous errors regarding which Scrivener said, "Erasmus' first edition is in that respect the faultiest book I know" (p. 296). Erasmus hated the tedium of proofreading and correcting his own books (Froude, p. 8).

REFORMATION:

Started in 1517 and ended in 1648. The Reformation lasted 131 years. Christians killing Christians

The Council of Trent was brought about to counter the Reformation. What was done?

1. They started the Catholic denomination in Christianity in 1559.
2. They started the Jesuit Order.

The Jesuits helped carry out two major objectives of the Counter-Reformation: The Jesuits established numerous schools and universities throughout Europe and pushed the supremacy of the Pope and Catholic church. WE STILL LIVE IN THE ERA OF THE COUNTER REFORMATION.

3. The Roman Catholic Church had its Latin Vulgate, which was done by Jerome. It was translated into the English LANGUAGE, AND THEY CALLED IT THE Douay-Rheims.

This was all done to counter the Reformation.

WHAT IS FUNNY ABOUT THE REFORMATION IS THE FACT THAT PEOPLE WANTED OUT FROM UNDER THE POPE'S AUTHORITY. WHAT THE REFORMATION DID WAS TO KEEP PEOPLE IN CHRISTIANITY AND DECEIVED. I believe the Reformation was started by the Papacy using Christian priests like Luther and others to start the protests against the Papacy. And led to the killing of Christians by Christians and gave the Papacy the power to make it happen, which led to the Counter-reformation by the Papacy. It also opened the door to bringing back a lot of the old pagan belief systems and led to the Jews returning to the Judaism that Yahweh had done away with.

1522, Luther's New Testament. - German. 1534, Tyndale's New Testament. - English.

1534 C.E., Luther's translation of the Old Testament.

1545 C.E., Tradition, sayings of Popes and Councils as equal to scriptures.

The Council of Trent (Latin: Concilium Tridentinum), held between 1545 and 1563 in Trent (or Trento, in northern Italy), was the 19th ecumenical council of the Catholic Church. Prompted by the Protestant Reformation, it has been described as the embodiment of the Counter-Reformation. Within that time, the Jesuits were started, the Catholic denomination in Christianity was started, and the Douey Rheims were the first Catholic scriptures put in English from Jerome's Latin Vulgate, all done to counter the Reformation.

The Council of Trent condemned every other translation of the scriptures except for the Latin Vulgate. "Moreover, the same sacred and holy Synod–considering that no small utility may accrue to the Church of God, if it is made known which out of all the Latin editions, now in circulation, of the sacred books, is to be held as authentic,–ordains and declares, that the said old and vulgate edition, which, by the lengthened usage of so many years, has been approved of in the Church, be, in public lectures, disputations, sermons and expositions, held as authentic; and that no one is to dare, or presume to reject it under any pretext whatever."

1546 C.E., Roman tradition was placed on the same level as Scripture.

1546 C.E., Apocrypha was received into the Canon.

1559 C.E., This is when the Catholic denomination, which was started for the Counter-Reformation, started.

CHAPTER 18
CATHOLIC CHURCH FATHERS ARE MADE-UP LIES

All these so-called Catholic Church fathers are made-up lies of Rome. IF ALL THE SO-CALLED CHURCH FATHERS WERE NOT KILLED DURING THE PERSECUTIONS IN THEIR LIFETIME, THEN THEY WERE NOT BELIEVERS IN YAHWEH MESSIAH, AND THEIR LIFE STORIES WERE ALL MADE UP:

NAME: DEATH DATE

1. IGNATIUS 140
2. POLYCARP 155
3. JUSTIN MARTYR 165
4. MELITO 180
5. IRENAEUS 202
6. TERTULLIAN 225
7. ORIGEN 254
8. COUNL 325 – The only one that lived during the 4th century. COMPARE THEIR DEATH DATES TO THE PERSECUTION TIMES.

Catholics say these guys were Christians who were martyred, so they could never have been part of Yahweh's Elect. Christianity was started in the 4th century by Constantine. The last (the 11th) persecution (of Constantine's) ended in 313.

Emperor/Date (A.D.)

1. Nero 54-68
2. Domitian 81-96
3. Trajan 98-117
4. Marcus Aurelius 161-180
5. Septimius Severus 193-211
6. Maximinus the Thracian 235-238
7. Decius Trajan 249-251
8. Valerian 253-260
9. Lucius Aurelian 270-275
10. Diocletian 284-305
11. Constantine ruled from 306-337

Roman Empire was changed to a religious government under Constantine.

Diocletian died in 305, and Constantine took over in 306, so Constantine continued Diocletian's Persecution as his own.

Constantine ruled from 306 to 337.

The last (the 11th) persecution (of Constantine's) ended in 313.

HOUSE OF CHRISTIANITY

Christians are all in a big house with over 38,000 to 44,000 rooms and each room is a different denomination. Where people try taking other people from one room to another. Non-Denomination people are in the Hallways of that house. All saying they are the ones with the real truth. If they would look up, they would see that they are all under the same roof, in the House of Christianity. Yahweh is the key to getting you out of that house. His truth is the only one that leads to salvation.

INHERITED LIES

"Those who stick to their inherited lies and yawn at the truth have no light in them nor a switch to turn it on."

By Gary W. Stanfield

CHAPTER 19
THE TRINITY IS A PAGAN LIE

The Trinity is a pagan lie. Constantine incorporated this teaching into his Christianity from his pagan belief system. The Spirit is the Father Yahweh. That takes care of the Father and Spirit. The Son is the Flesh, and the Father Yahweh, who is Spirit, put His Spirit or Himself into the Flesh fully, thus Yahweh the Father in the Flesh, Yahweh Messiah. Yahweh is ONE. He put on the flesh to dwell among men and to become the offered Lamb. He revealed Himself through the Flesh and the Spirit.

The first thing Yahweh did in Creation was to make flesh for Himself to dwell in, and this is how we were made after His image. Scriptures were corrupted by Constantine and Jerome, the biggest culprits among others. There are no originals unless the Vatican is sitting on them, which is why through study, people are trying to bring about more truth from them. The Roman Empire, under Constantine and others, had over one thousand years—14, 25, or 40 generations of people, depending on how many years make a generation (some say 70 years, 40 years, and 25 years)—to perpetuate the lie of the name Jesus Christ. The following is how it was done:

1. Mixed pagan religions with Judaism = Christianity.
2. Added pagan holidays like Christmas and Easter to influence pagans to come over to Christianity.
3. Collected all existing manuscripts and had anyone killed who possessed them.
4. Took Yahweh's name out of the Scriptures, the only name for salvation, and filled the Scriptures with all kinds of pagan deity names and pagan words from paganism.

5. Took the truth of Scriptures and made them a lie, mostly by putting pagan deity names and words into Scriptures to make them more acceptable to the pagan culture and to the uneducated masses to come over to Christianity.

6. Put Scriptures in a language the common and uneducated did not know (Latin) and taught it.

7. Had anyone who did not convert to Christianity was killed because it was the only religion allowed at that time.

8. Constantine and many persecutors before and after him had many book burnings to hide the truth.

9. All books were rewritten during that time, and there were many forgeries, which is why you hear about so many lost books. By doing this, they also changed history from what it really was. I believe Constantine did not get rid of any books or add any since he was the one who propagandized the scriptures, so from doing that, he had no reason to add or subtract any books. The Papacy has changed the histories of many countries just to cover up the Christian lie. Even the truth of the Scriptures was made a lie. What Pagan Rome has done with their Christianity is to make the Scriptures the "Word of God," which made void the "Word of Yahweh," rendering the Scriptures void of salvation, and they know this.

CHRISTIANITY MADE FOR A PURPOSE

No religion or church will change a nation.

They are all built on the wrong foundation.

Yes, religion is an all-man-made prevarication.

They are found on every continent and nation.

Christianity was created to deceive man,

Such a big part of Satan's deceitful plan.

To deliver the world and men into his hand,

Yahweh's plan of salvation is to save man.

Yahweh Messiah is a Faith, not a religion

One day, you will have to make a decision.

This is what will cause the end-time division.

When Christianity becomes the world religion.

Immanuel; born to become Yahweh in the flesh.

The truth will be given to man all afresh,

Then wheat from the chaff will Yahweh thresh.

The elect will be taken, those left, burning flesh.

By Gary W. Stanfield

CHAPTER 20
CONSTANTINE'S PROPAGANDIZED NEW COVENANT

SCRIPTURES along with other history of what happened to the Word of Yahweh. The story of the Scriptures.

I have a huge notebook proving the name Yahweh from all kinds of different resources. Yahweh means "I am that I am"; in other words, He has always existed. There is no original Word of Yahweh texts unless the Vatican is sitting on them. They still have Constantine's copies, which were done from the original Hebrew, so it seems they should also have the originals in some form. Constantine created the office of bishop because they were actually pagan priests from the pagan religions. They took Yahweh's name out of the texts and put pagan deity names back in to make them void of salvation and more appealing to the pagans. He had 50 scriptures made and called them the New Testimonies in 331 C.E. This is how they started calling the Old and New Covenant the Old and New Testament. Constantine only did the New Covenant, not the Old, in Greek. Then Jerome came along, ordered by Bishop Damascus to write a new translation into Latin, and it became known as Jerome's Latin Vulgate, with the Old and New propagandized Covenants then being called the Old and New Testaments in 400 C.E., adding more paganism to the word of Yahweh. Jerome's Latin Vulgate was the only scripture available for over 1,000 years, locked up in the Latin tongue, which the common person did not know. Wycliffe, Tyndale, and Luther all started out with the Latin Vulgate and then used each other's translations. The King James root is also the Latin Vulgate, which is why it has so many Latin words within it. I grew up with the KJV, so I am very used to it. But what I have done is put the right names back or words as I have studied for the truth of it all. When you study history, you can eventually get a knack for discerning what is true and what is false. It's the Christian writings that I have found that keep the lies of history going to cover up what they are and what they have done throughout history. I have read so many history books; I collect them, especially religious histories, to compare with each other.

For instance, when the Four Horsemen of the first four Seals were opened to me, it was the third Seal with the Black Horse and Balances with "hurt not the oil and the wine" that was opened first to me. I was reading those verses one night, and it hit me from my love of history that Greece could only grow grapes and olives and not much else. So, I dug some history books out and started reading. Sure enough, the Grecian Empire was a trading empire because they could not grow much wheat and barley; they had to trade for it, and hence the balances. All they really had to trade was olive oil and wine/grapes and olives. So, the rider had to be Alexander the Great, who started the Grecian Empire, but everything fit. So, I thought, if that is true, then the second Red Horse Seal must be Medo-Persia, which all came together. Then, the first Seal had to be the Babylonian Empire, which panned out, and the fourth then had to be the Roman Empire. The riders of the Pale Horse were Death, the Emperors of the 10 Roman persecutions that killed off the Elect of Yahweh. It's a neat feeling when things like that happen. No one else has ever taught them that way, yet they are proven by scriptures and history. Yes, salvation was to the Hebrew people first and came through the tribe of Judah. What they actually call original Greek today is from Erasmus in the 1500s, which I believe was taught to hide the fact of what Constantine did with those he had done in Greek. You must think about how many generations of people there are in over 1,000 years. That's why the Dark Ages were called the Dark Ages. No one knows the whole truth and never will until the Seven-Year Peace Plan. The very reason why Yahweh is sending Moses and Eliyah to bring that truth back is because the Word of Yahweh was made a lie, and that was supposed to happen. But the darker this world gets, the more light is given, so there is enough truth being given to show people that all these world religions and Christianity are nothing but lies of Satan. Also, through the mercies of Yahweh, all mankind will hear the truth and have the opportunity to believe it or not. No matter what people have done in this world under Satan's influence, they all have a chance to be forgiven. Yahweh has made a way for all the people who have died without hearing the whole truth and without salvation being available to have the opportunity to obtain it, and for those who are alive during the Papacy's 7-Year Peace Plan.

Jeremiah 31:31 Behold, the days come, saith Yahweh, that I will make a New Covenant with the house of Judaea, and with the house of Judah:

Jeremiah 50:5 "Come and let us join ourselves to Yahweh in a perpetual covenant that will not be forgotten."

Ephesians 2:13-14

13 But now in Messiah Yahweh ye who sometimes were far off are made nigh the blood of Yahweh

14 For he is our peace, who hath made both one, and hath broken down the middle wall of partition between us;

Luke 22:20 Likewise also the cup after supper, saying, this cup [is] the New Covenant in my blood, which is shed for you.

Hebrews 9:15 And for this because he is the mediator of the New Covenant, that by means of death, for the redemption of the transgressions that were under the First Covenant, they which are called might receive the promise of eternal inheritance.

2 Corinthians 3:6 - Who also hath made us able ministers of the New Covenant; not of the letter, but of the Spirit: for the letter killed, but the Spirit giveth life.

Luke 22:20 Likewise also the cup after supper, saying, this cup [is] the New Covenant in my blood, which is shed for you.

Constantine, in 331 A.D., had 50 of his pagan scriptures done in the GREEK and the only ones allowed at that time.

The Fifty Scriptures of Constantine were scriptures in Greek taken from the Hebrew, called the Word of Yahweh;

Acts 6:7 "And the Word of Yahweh increased."

Acts 12:24 "But the Word of Yahweh grew and multiplied."

Hebrews 4:12 "For the Word of Yahweh is quick, and powerful, and sharper than any two-edged sword, piercing even to the dividing asunder of soul and spirit, and of the joints and marrow, and is a discerner of the thoughts and intents of the heart."

AS YOU CAN SEE, A CHANGE TOOK PLACE WITH THE WORD OF YAHWEH. They were commissioned in 331 by Constantine and prepared by Eusebius of Caesarea. He ordered the destruction of the writings of any opposition and the immediate execution by the sword of any citizens preserving illegal literature, either by hiding or secreting scrolls or codices.

ACTS 10:36-37

36 The word which YAHWEH sent unto the children of Judaea, teaching peace, the Word by Yahweh Messiah: (he is the master of all)

³⁷ That word, I say, ye know, which was published throughout all (Judaea), and began from Galilee, after the baptism which John taught.

Deuteronomy 17:2-3

² If there is found among you, within any of your gates which Yahweh your Almighty gives you, a man or a woman who has been wicked in the sight of Yahweh your Almighty, in transgressing His Covenant.

³ Who has gone and served other deities and worshiped them, either the sun or moon or any of the host of heaven, which I have not commanded,

Constantine von Tischendorf, the discoverer of Codex Sinaiticus, found the world's oldest and most complete Bible in 1844, dating to around the mid-4th century. It is called Codex Sinaiticus after Saint Catharine's Monastery at Mount Sinai, where Tischendorf discovered it. He believed that Sinaiticus and Vaticanus were among the fifty Bibles prepared by Eusebius in Caesarea for Constantine. According to him, they were written with three (as Vaticanus) or four columns per page (as Sinaiticus). Tischendorf's view was supported by Pierre Batiffol, a Catholic priest. Codex Sinaiticus and Codex Vaticanus, two of the great uncial codices representing the Alexandrian text-type, are considered excellent manuscript witnesses of the text of the New Testament. Most critical editions of the Greek New Testament give precedence to these two chief uncial manuscripts, and most translations are based on their text. Sinaiticus is younger than Vaticanus by at least 50 years.

I heard a priest on the radio on March 16, 2022, say that he got to see the oldest complete Bible in existence today, with all the books, made in 332 A.D., when he was in the Vatican Library. Then he mentioned Constantine and said that Constantine had 50 scriptures made, but he did not mention anything about Constantine having them done in Greek. If they still have Constantine's, then they would be holding on to the originals that Constantine used to put his scriptures into Greek, it seems.

Constantine put the Word of Yahweh into Greek from the original Hebrew. Jerome put Constantine's Greek scriptures into Latin. Erasmus put Jerome's Latin back into Greek, which they are calling the original Greek.

Galatians 1:6-7

6 I marvel that ye are so soon removed from him that called you into the kingdom of Yahweh unto another Word:

7 Which is not another; but there be some that trouble you and would pervert the Word of Yahweh.

According to Eusebius, Constantine wrote him in his letter:

I have thought it expedient to instruct your Prudence to order fifty copies of the sacred Scriptures, the provision and use of which you know to be most needful for the instruction of the Church, to be written on prepared parchment in a legible manner and in a convenient, portable form, by professional transcribers thoroughly practiced in their art. These orders, said Eusebius, were followed by the immediate execution of the work itself we sent him [Constantine] magnificently and elaborately bound volumes of three-fold and four-fold forms (Life of Constantine, vol. iv, p.36). They were the New Testimonies, and this is the first mention (c. 331) of the New Testament in the historical record. With his instructions fulfilled, Constantine then decreed that the New Testimonies would thereafter be called the word of the Roman Saviour God and official to all presbyters sermonizing in the Roman Empire. (Life of Constantine, vol. iii, p. 29)

In a remarkable aside, the Church further admits that "the earliest of the extant manuscripts [of the New Testament], it is true, do not date back beyond the middle of the fourth century A.D." (Catholic Encyclopedia, op. cit., pp. 656-7).

NOTE: SACRED, A SUN DEITY NAME IS ANOTHER ADDITION TO THE OLD AND NEW TESTAMENTS / COVENANTS, SO PAGANISM KEPT ADDING MORE LIES TO THE SCRIPTURES. THE PAPACY IS IN FULL CONTROL.

JEROME'S PROPAGANDIZED OLD COVENANT THAT HE RENAMED THE OLD TESTAMENT: JEROME'S LATIN VULGATE in 405 A.D. Jerome put Constantine's Greek propagandized translation of the New Covenant into Latin, which Constantine had renamed the New Testament, what is called today the New Testament. Starting in the year 382 C.E., it became known as Jerome's Latin Vulgate. At the same time, Jerome put the Hebrew Old Covenant into Latin, beginning in about 390 C.E., and followed Constantine's lead by renaming it the Old Testament and propagandizing it too. With some certainty, the first widespread edition of the Scriptures was assembled by Jerome around 400 C.E. for the New and 390 C.E. for the Old, the first scriptures to have both the Old and New Covenant/Testament, both done in Latin, which Jerome named the Bible. These were the only scriptures available for over one thousand years, locked up in the Latin tongue, which the common person did not know. This became known as Jerome's Latin Vulgate. You must remember that the Jews were also part of the Roman Empire and were forced to become Christians or die. The Vulgate was created due to the efforts of Jerome, whose translation was declared to be the authentic Latin version of the Bible by the Council of Trent. This is where the Catholic Douay Rheims translation came from, put into English by members of the English College Douai in the service of the Catholic Church.

NOTE: JEHOVAH IS A WORD THAT DID NOT EXIST UNTIL THE 16TH CENTURY AND CAME FROM GERMANY AND A GERMAN PRIEST. THIS WORD WAS ADDED LATER IN THE OLD COVENANT WAY AFTER JEROME HAD ALREADY PROPAGANDIZED THEM.

Even though Constantine changed the Roman Empire's form of government from secular over religious to religious over secular, he did not start the "Holy Roman Empire." There never was one. It stayed in the Roman Empire until 932, which is when they started calling it the "Holy Roman Empire"; this was done for deceit. We are still living in the era of the Roman Empire, the last empire, but not in its final form; the emperors were exchanged for the Popes.

CHAPTER 21
CONSTANTINE REVEALED WHO THE BEAST, ANTI-MESSIAH, ETC. ARE

Constantine revealed who the Beast, the man of transgressions, is, the son of Perdition, and who the false prophet is, as well as the Anti-Messiah. The Beast is the Papacy; all the others pertain to the Pope.

2 Thessalonians 2:3

3 Let no man deceive you by any means: for that day shall not come, except there comes a falling away first, and that man of transgression be revealed, the son of perdition. (The Pope)

"Except there comes a falling away first." The persecution lasted 247 years.

The falling away took place during the 11 Roman emperor persecutions, and they revealed that it was the Pontifex Maximus / Pope since all the emperors held that title by being over religious and secular governments, so you can see how that played into Constantine's hands.

Luke 24:47-49

47 "And that repentance and remission of transgressions should be taught in His name to all nations, HIS NAME IS YAHWEH, THEY ARE NOT TEACHING HIS NAME TODAY, IT IS ONLY ANTI-MESSIAH NAMES THEY ALL USE AND TEACH. And if they use Yahweh's name it is not used for the Messiah's name.

159

⁴⁸ And you are witnesses of these things.

⁴⁹ And, behold, I send the promise of my Father upon you: but tarry ye in the city of Zion, until ye be endued with power from on high.

Acts 1:4,5,8 And, being assembled together with them, commanded them that they should not depart from Zion, but wait for the promise of the Father, which, saith he, ye have heard of me. 5 For John truly baptized with water; but ye shall be baptized with the Spirit not many days hence.8. But ye shall receive power, after that the Spirit is come upon you: and ye shall be witnesses unto me both in Zion, and in all Judea, and in Samaria, and unto the uttermost part of the earth

Matt. 28:19 Go ye therefore, and teach all nations, baptizing them in the name of the Father, and of the Son, and of the Spirit (Yahweh):

Mark 16:15-20

¹⁵ And he said unto them, Go ye into all the world, and teach the word to every creature.

¹⁶ He that believes and is baptized shall be saved; but he that believes not shall be condemned.

The above verse speaking about baptism is not speaking of water baptism, but the baptism of the Spirit. How do we know this?

Acts 1:8 But ye shall receive power, after that the Spirit is come upon you: and ye shall be witnesses unto me both in Zion, and in all Judaea, and in Samaria, and unto the uttermost part of the earth.

Now read verses 17 and 18 below. These two verses that follow verse 16 prove that the baptism that is being spoken about is the baptism of the Spirit, which is what gives a person salvation, and verse 20 confirms it with signs.

17 And these signs shall follow them that believe; In my name shall they cast out devils; they shall speak with new tongues;

18 They shall take up serpents; and if they drink any deadly thing, it shall not hurt them; they shall lay hands on the sick and they shall recover. (Notice: It does not say MIGHT but Shall.)

19 So then after Yahweh Messiah had spoken unto them, he was received up into heaven, and sat on the right hand of Yahweh. (Remember, scriptures speak of only one throne not two.)

20 And they went forth, and taught everywhere, Yahweh working with them, and confirming the word with signs following.

Matthew 3:11

"As for me, I baptize you with water for repentance, but He who is coming after me is mightier than I, and I am not fit to remove His sandals; He will baptize you with the Spirit and fire.

Mark 1:8 I baptized you with water, but He will baptize you with the Spirit."

In the next verse, Paul says that the Word was taught to every creature under heaven. BACK THEN!

Colossians 1:23 If ye continue in the faith grounded and settled and be not moved away from the hope of the word, which ye have heard, and which was taught to every creature which is under the heaven; whereof I Paul am made minister. (Notice Paul did not make himself a teacher, but he says, "He was made a teacher." This could only have come from Yahweh.)

This proves that Christianity is a lie.

161

In Christianity, you have Preachers and priests, going to colleges and seminaries to learn how to preach and learn what their denomination teaches. This is to ensure that when they become preachers, they are within their own denominational walls. But Yahweh teaches His elect all things and why seminaries are against Yahweh's Word.

Mark 16:16 He that believeth and is baptized shall be saved; but he that believeth not shall be damned.

You see, the entire world back then had a choice to BELIEVE or NOT TO BELIEVE. OUR ANCESTORS WERE THE ONES WHO DID NOT BELIEVE, AND TODAY, WE INHERITED THEIR LIES. THE FALLING AWAY TOOK PLACE BACK THEN, DURING THE PERSECUTIONS.

Revelation 19:20-21

"And the beast was taken, and with him the false prophet that wrought miracles before him, with which he deceived them that had received the mark of the beast, and them that worshipped his image. These both were cast alive into a lake of fire burning with brimstone."

I BELIEVE THE WHITE POPE WILL BE OVER THE WORLD RELIGION, AND THE BLACK POPE WILL BE OVER THE WORLD GOVERNMENT, RULING FROM ZION.

"ROME WHEN IN MINORITY IS AS GENTLE AS A LAMB, WHEN IN EQUALITY IS AS CLEVER AS A FOX AND WHEN IN THE MAJORITY IS AS FIERCE AS A TIGER"

YOU SHALL SEE

In time, the entire world shall see,

A One World Government there shall be.

Ruled by no one else but the Papacy.

Proven by history and by prophecy.

The Pope cannot wait to take his throne,

When in Zion, he shall be shown.

That is when people will moan and groan,

When this deceitful truth is finally sown.

Then the entire world shall see,

What the Mark of the Beast will be.

Many will think it will set them free,

But this will start the killing spree.

By Gary W. Stanfield

Constantine started the Papacy form of government when he became the first Pope over the pagan religion of Christianity and changed the Roman Empire's secular government to a religious government. He had started from an already existing pagan religion by the same name. Now, why would he have done this? It was done for deceit because he had killed off the last of the Elect of Yahweh Messiah, and all that was left were the pagans, our ancestors, and we inherited their lies.

Daniel 7:21 I beheld, and the same horn made war with the elect, and prevailed against them;

While Judah denotes a specific tribe and its associated kingdom, Judea represents a broader geopolitical territory. Judea lost its independence to the Romans in the 1st century B.C. THEIR COVER-UP TRICK IS THAT JACOB WAS NAMED ISRAEL OR JUDAH AND NOT JUDEA. YAHWEH TOLD JACOB HE WOULD BECOME A GREAT NATION, SO THE NATION WOULD BE NAMED AFTER HIM, JUDEA, AND NOT JUDAH, HIS SON'S NAME.

Emperor Hadrian and Zion/Jerusalem, along with Judaea.

66-70 C.E. & 132- 135 C.E. were the Jewish revolts.

Hadrian permanently banned Jews from setting foot in Zion and then rebuilt the city as a Roman colony. The Zion of today is not the Zion that the Messiah walked.

Palestine, which Roman Emperor Hadrian placed on the country of Judaea in 135C.E.

A letter inserted in the Augustan History, ascribed to the Emperor Hadrian, refers to the worship of Serapis by residents of Egypt who described themselves as Christians: "The land of Egypt, the praises of which you have been recounting to me, my dear Servianus, I have found to be wholly light-minded, unstable, and blown about by every breath of rumor. There, those who worship Serapis are, in fact, Christians, and those who call themselves Bishops of Christ are, in fact, devotees of Serapis.

Genesis 32:28 And he said, thy name shall be called no more Jacob, but Judaea: for as a prince hast thou power with Yahweh and with men, and hast prevailed.

What made me check the name Israel out is the fact that the name asks a question, Is Ra El? (Amen Ra). And it hit me that Yahweh would not name Jacob after some pagan sun deity. Just like naming the baby Jesus after Zeus, changing it from Immanuel, which was the name given to him. Yahweh is called Amen in the following verse, which is another pagan lie.

Revelation 3:14 "And unto the Messenger of the assembly of the Laodiceans write; These things saith the Amen, the faithful and true witness, the beginning of the creation of Yahweh;"

Constantine wanted to unify all the pagans under one religion, that of Christianity. The Roman Empire at that time engulfed the whole of humanity, including Judaea or Judea, the modern spelling. Emperor Hadrian named the area of Judea Palestine, it was not until after WW2 that they named Judea Israel. During WW2, the British were sinking ships full of Jews trying to go back to their homeland until the League of Nations told Britain that it was ok for them to go back. The Pope was over the League of Nations just like he is over the U.N. today and will be over the end-times World Union. Israel, as the nation's name was planted incredibly early in time in the scriptures, was not there originally for these latter days of deceit. So, through Satan, this was all preplanned. The following verses prove it all.

Acts 10:36-37 King James Version

36 The word which Yahweh sent unto the children of (Judaea), teaching the Word of Yahweh Messiah: (he is Master of all:)

37 That word, I say, ye know, which was published throughout all (Judaea), and began from Galilee, after the baptism which John taught.

Revelation 13:7-10

It was also given to him to make war with the Elect and to overcome them, and authority over every tribe and people and tongue and nation was given to him. All who dwell on the earth will worship him, everyone whose name has not been written from the foundation of the world in the book of life of the Lamb who has been slain. If anyone has an ear, let him hear.

This is when the lies were started and perpetuated. Constantine took the Word of Yahweh and put it into Greek, taken from the original Hebrew, propagandized them, and made them void of salvation.

Q. CONSTANTINE REVEALED WHAT THE MARK OF THE BEAST/PAPACY WOULD BE:

312 C.E., Constantine and the Battle of the Milvian Bridge, where he saw the cross in the sky and was told to, "IN THIS SIGN CONQUER." Crusades = War of the Cross. Rome became PAPAL Rome on October 28, 312 A.D., when Constantine exchanged the eagle for the cross: The cross is not only a sun symbol but also a symbol of Christianity. Constantine was a pagan sun worshiper.

The last Pope during the 3 ½ year Tribulation Period will make Christianity the World Religion and have anyone killed who will not come over to it. People will take the Mark to save their lives. The only ones that will not are the Spirit-filled Elect of Yahweh Messiah at that time.

This PAPACY BABYLONIAN GOVERNMENT SYSTEM that is of Satan is what Yahweh will destroy at His coming.

"ROME; WHEN IN MINORITY IS AS GENTLE AS A LAMB, WHEN IN EQUALITY IS AS CLEVER AS A FOX, AND WHEN IN THE MAJORITY IS AS FIERCE AS A TIGER."

Revelation 14:9-10

Then another Messenger, a third one, followed them, saying with a loud voice, "If anyone worships the beast and his image and receives a mark on his forehead or on his hand, he also will drink of the wine of the wrath of Yahweh, which is mixed in full strength in the cup of His anger; and he will be tormented with fire and brimstone in the presence of the righteous Messengers and in the presence of the Lamb."

Revelation 13:16

And he causes all, the small and the great, and the rich and the poor, and the freemen and the slaves, to be given a mark on their right hand or on their forehead.

Revelation 13:17

And he provides that no one will be able to buy or to sell, except the one who has the mark, either the name of the beast or the number of his name. People will take the Mark to save their lives.

S. IMAGE OF THE BEAST/PAPACY: THE POPE

NOTE: It will not be the House of Yahweh that the Pope sits in. It will be the Dome of the Rock, which was built by Constantine and is the nickname for the Temple of God, which was its name in the first place. That is what Constantine named it when he built it in the 4th century. Dome of the Rock became its nickname. Yahweh did away with the House of Yahweh worship and animal offerings, the Levite priesthood, tithing, and what we call Judaism. So, there is no need for a House of Yahweh as far as Yahweh is concerned. He will build a new one during the Millennial Kingdom himself, the 3rd one.

2 Thessalonians 2:1-16

¹ Now we beseech you, brethren, by the coming of our Master Yahweh Messiah, and by our gathering together unto Him,

² That ye be not soon shaken in mind, or be troubled, neither by spirit, nor by word, nor by letter as from us, as that the day of Yahweh is at hand.

³ Let no man beguile you in any wise; for, except the falling away come first, and the man of transgression be revealed the son of perdition,

⁴ He that opposes and exalts himself against all that is called a deity or that is worshipped; so that he sits in the temple of a deity, setting himself forth as a deity.

⁵ Don't you remember, that, when I was yet with you, I told you these things?

⁶ And now you know which restrains, to the end that he (Pontifex Maximus) may be revealed in his own season.

⁷ For the mystery of lawlessness already works only there is one that restrains now (the Spirit), until he be taken out of the way.

⁸ And then shall that Wicked be revealed, whom Yahweh shall consume with the spirit of his mouth, and shall destroy with the brightness of His coming:

⁹ Even him (POPE), whose coming is after the working of Satan with all power and signs and lying wonders,

¹⁰ And with all deceivableness of unrighteousness in them that perish; because they received not the love of the truth, that they might be saved.

¹¹ And for this cause Yahweh shall send them strong delusion, that they should believe a lie:

¹² That they all might be damned who believed not the truth but had pleasure in unrighteousness.

¹³ But we are bound to give thanks always to Yahweh for you, brethren beloved of Yahweh, because Yahweh hath from the beginning chosen you to salvation through the infilling of the Spirit and belief of the truth:

¹⁴ Whereunto he called you by our word, to the obtaining of the Spirit of our Master Yahweh Messiah.

¹⁵ Therefore, brethren, stand fast, and hold the truth which ye have been taught, whether by word, or our epistle.

¹⁶ Now our Master Yahweh Messiah Himself, and Yahweh, even our Father, which hath loved us, and hath given us everlasting consolation and good hope through the Spirit,

1 John 2:18 Little children, it is the last time: and as ye have heard that anti- Messiah shall come, even now are there many anti-messiahs; whereby we know that it is the last time.

Paul told the believers back then what the restrainer was. I believe it wasn't put into the Scriptures, so it could be revealed again for the last-day prophecies. But it was also kept quiet because 2 Thessalonians, Chapter 1, shows that they were being persecuted by the Roman Empire at that time.

The spirit-filled knew the truth because Yahweh taught His elect all things where no man needed to teach them, but there were many who believed the truth who were not yet filled with the Spirit of Yahweh.

1 Thessalonians 3:1-8, 14-15

¹ Therefore, when we could endure it no longer, we thought it best to be left behind at Athens alone,

² and we sent Timothy, our brother and Yahweh's fellow worker in the truth of the Messiah, to strengthen and encourage you as to your faith,

³ so that no one would be disturbed by these afflictions; for you yourselves know that we have been destined for this.

⁴ For indeed when we were with you, we kept telling you in advance that we were going to suffer affliction; and so it came to pass, as you know.

⁵ For this reason, when I could endure it no longer, I also sent to find out about your faith, for fear that the tempter might have tempted you, and our labor would be in vain.

⁶ But now that Timothy has come to us from you, and has brought us good news of your faith and love, and that you always think kindly of us, longing to see us just as we also long to see you,

⁷ for this reason, in all our distress and affliction we were comforted about you through your faith;

⁸ For now, we really live, if you stand firm in Yahweh.

¹⁴ "For you, brethren, became imitators of the assemblies of Yahweh in Messiah Yahweh that are in Judea, for you also endured the same sufferings at the hands of your own countrymen, even as they did from the Jews,"

¹⁵ "who both killed the Messiah and the prophets, and drove us out. They are not pleasing to Yahweh, but hostile to all men,"

Matthew 23:34-37

34 Wherefore, behold, I send unto you prophets, and wise men, and scribes: and some of them ye shall kill; and some of them shall ye scourge in your House of Yahweh, and persecute them from city to city.

35 That upon you may come all the righteous blood shed upon the earth, from the blood of righteous Abel unto the blood of Zacharias son of Barachias, whom ye slew between the House of Yahweh and the altar.

36 Verily I say unto you, All these things shall come upon this generation.

37 O Zion, Zion, thou that killest the prophets, and stonest them which are sent unto thee, how often would I have gathered thy children together, even as a hen gathereth her chickens under her wings, and ye would not!

LIFE AND LETTERS OF ST. PAUL BY DAVID SMITH, NO COPYRIGHT BUT CA. 1930 - PAGE 178, 179

That imagination of Jewish eschatology was familiar to Paul's mind, and it furnished him with a cogent argument against the excesses of the Thessalonian enthusiasts. The Second Advent was indeed imminent.

The glorious consummation was at hand, but it would not immediately arrive. It would be heralded by two world-shaking preliminaries—the dissolution of the Roman Empire and the appearance of the Anti-Christ [Messiah]; and neither of these had yet come to pass.

The Little Horn of Daniel 7:25 would come from the Roman Empire, and then it would be changed. This Little Horn or Anti-Messiah [Constantine] would change it to a religious government.

This person is none other than the Pope. The Pope/Papacy is the only one that fulfills all the prophecies of the Anti-Messiah and Beast. The Roman Empire was changed over to a religious government, and the Papacy as a religious government could not come into existence until Constantine changed it from secular over religious power to religious over secular power.

PART B: The falling happened during the 11 Roman Emperor persecutions. Christianity wants you to believe it did not happen back then but is a future thing, but it has already happened.

Revelation 13:15

"And he had power to give life unto the image of the beast, that the image of the beast should both speak, and cause that as many as would not worship the image of the beast should be killed."

CHAPTER 22
THE ABOMINATION OF DESOLATION

Constantine built the Temple that the last Pope will move his throne to and who will be over the world religion of Christianity at that time, so he helped to fulfill that prophecy by what he had done building the Temple of God.

THE INSIDE OF THE "TEMPLE OF GOD" BUILT BY CONSTANTINE. THE VERY REASON WHY CHRISTIANS HAVE BEEN BRAINWASHED TO CALL THE HOUSE OF YAHWEH THE TEMPLE OF GOD. THERE WILL NOT BE A THIRD HOUSE OF YAHWEH UNTIL HIS MILLENNIAL KINGDOM. THIS IS WHERE THE POPE WILL MOVE HIS THRONE.

There is no mention of a ROCK when Abraham was going to offer Isaac in Genesis chapter 22.

Genesis 22:9 And they came to the place which Yahweh had told him of; and ABRAHAM BUILT AN ALTAR THERE and LAID THE WOOD IN ORDER, and bound Isaac, his son, and LAID HIM ON THE ALTAR UPON THE WOOD.

Absolutely not one huge rock; Abraham built the altar himself.

Matthew 24:15

"Therefore, when you see the ABOMINATION OF DESOLATION which was spoken of through Daniel the prophet, standing in the righteous place (let the reader understand).

The Abomination of Desolation is when the Pope moves his throne to the Temple of God, built by Constantine in the 4th century. It is inside the façade of the Dome of the Rock, and the Dome is the roof of the Temple inside. The Temple is Roman architecture, not Muslim. The Temple of God will be used by the Muslims, Christians, and the Jews.

The Muslim Sabbath is on Friday, the Jewish Sabbath is on Saturday, and the Christian Sabbath is on Sunday. It will work out that they will all have their day to use it, with the Pope overseeing everything. The Muslims pray on the floor; the Jews pray to the wall; The Christians pray to the ceiling. The Muslim symbol is the moon, the Jewish symbol is the star, and the Christian symbol is the Cross that represents the sun. There are only Muslim Mosques; Jewish Synagogues, and Christian churches, no Protestant ones. In Zion today, this should show Christians that the Papacy will get rid of all denominations in Christianity, even the Catholic ones, and there will only be the religion of Christianity that wins out.

1 Thessalonians 2:4

"Who opposeth and exalteth himself above all that is called a deity, or that is worshipped; so that he as a deity sitteth in the temple of God, shewing himself that he is a deity."

Revelation 11:1-2

And there was given me a reed like unto a rod: and the angel/Messenger stood, saying, Rise, and measure the Temple of God, and the altar, and them that worship therein. But the court which is without the temple leave out, and measure it not; for it is given unto the Gentiles: and Zion shall they tread under foot forty and two months. (3 ½ years)

IF THE COURT IS GIVEN TO THE GENTILES, THEN THE "TEMPLE OF GOD," WHICH IS SPOKEN OF LITERALLY ALSO BELONG TO THEM. THE MUSLIMS, JEWS, AND CHRISTIANS WILL

SHARE THE "TEMPLE OF GOD" DURING THE FIRST HALF OF THE 7-YEAR PEACE PLAN. THE PAPACY WILL MAKE CHRISTIANITY THE WORLD RELIGION AND ABSORB ALL THE OTHER ONES IN THE LAST 3 ½ YEARS OF THE PEACE PLAN.

The Jews never used anything called a Temple; those who worshiped the sun did. The Jews used the House of Yahweh. In fact, Jews never used anything called a Synagogue / Sin-a-God are two pagan moon deity names like Allah is; those that worshiped the moon did. The Jews were all Christians, too. Constantine made Christianity the Catholic/Universal State religion of the Roman Empire and killed anyone who would not become a Christian, just like what will happen during the coming Tribulation Period. All this talk about a Temple being rebuilt in Jerusalem by the Jews will never happen. More deceit to keep people engaged in the lies.

Jacob was not named Israel by Yahweh but Judaea, and one of his sons name was Judah. They tried using Judah and Israel to perpetuate their lie. Judah had his own country, and Judaea engulfed all the tribes.

The name Zion, the City of David, was changed to Jerusalem; in many verses, Sion is used instead of Zion. Sion refers to the sun. Yahweh's word was hidden with lies, but those who are willing to do some deep studies outside the walls of Christianity will find the truth that will lead them to salvation in the end by showing themselves approved.

Genesis 22:9 And they came to the place which Yahweh had told him of; and ABRAHAM BUILT AN ALTAR THERE and LAID THE WOOD IN ORDER, and bound Isaac, his son, and LAID HIM ON THE ALTAR UPON THE WOOD.

Absolutely not one huge rock; Abraham built the altar himself.

- One more thing; it was Constantine and his mother who built these Christian churches on top of religious sites. Some had bigger churches built on the sites, tearing down the ones Constantine had built?
- The House of Yahweh was destroyed in 70 C.E.

The terms "A.D." and "B.C." have their roots in Christianity. "A.D." stands for anno domini (Latin for "in the year of the lord"), and it refers specifically to the birth of Jesus. "B.C." stands for "before Christ" (It comes from the Papacy).

ZION'S JUDGMENT TAKES PLACE IN ONE HOUR, AND THE FOLLOWING VERSES ARE WHY: SHE IS THE WOMAN, THE GREAT CITY; THE PAPACY IS THE BEAST.

Revelation 17:

¹ One of the seven Messengers who had the seven bowls came and said to me, "Come, I will show you the punishment of the great prostitute, who sits by many waters.

² With her the kings of the earth committed adultery, and the inhabitants of the earth were intoxicated with the wine of her adulteries."

³ Then the Messenger carried me away in the Spirit into a wilderness. There I saw a woman sitting on a scarlet beast that was covered with blasphemous names and had seven heads and ten horns.

⁴ The woman was dressed in purple and scarlet, and was glittering with gold, precious stones, and pearls. She held a golden cup in her hand, filled with abominable things and the filth of her adulteries.

⁵ The name written on her forehead was a mystery:

BABYLON THE GREAT

THE MOTHER OF PROSTITUTES

AND OF THE ABOMINATIONS OF THE EARTH

Revelation 18:4 And I heard another voice from heaven, saying, Come out of her (Zion with the Babylonian religious system as world religion and the Pope moved his throne there.), my people, that ye be not partakers of her transgressions, and that ye receive not of her plagues.

6 I saw that the woman was drunk with the blood of Yahweh's people, the blood of those who bore testimony to Yahweh Messiah. When I saw her, I was greatly astonished.

7 Then the Messenger said to me: "Why are you astonished? I will explain to you the mystery of the woman and of the beast she rides, which has the seven heads and ten horns.

8 The beast, which you saw, once was, now is not, and yet will come up out of the Abyss and go to its destruction. The inhabitants of the earth whose names have not been written in the book of life from the creation of the world will be astonished when they see the beast, because it once was, now is not, and yet will come.

9 "This calls for a mind with wisdom. The seven heads are seven hills on which the woman sits.

ZION SITS ON 7 HILLS.

10 They are also seven kings. Five have fallen, one is, the other has not yet come; but when he does come, he must remain for only a little while.

[11] The beast who once was, and now is not, is an eighth king. He belongs to the seven and is going to his destruction.

[12] "The ten horns you saw are ten kings who have not yet received a kingdom, but who for one hour will receive authority as kings along with the beast.

[13] They have one purpose and will give their power and authority to the beast.

[14] They will wage war against the Lamb, but the Lamb will triumph over them because he is King of kings— and with him will be his called, chosen and faithful followers."

[15] Then he said to me, "The waters which you saw, where the harlot sits, are peoples, multitudes, nations, and tongues.

[16] And the ten horns which you saw on the beast, these will hate the harlot, make her desolate and naked, eat her flesh and burn her with fire.

[17] For Yahweh has put it into their hearts to fulfill His purpose, to be of one mind, and to give their kingdom to the beast, until the words of Yahweh are fulfilled.

[18] And the woman whom you saw is that great city which reigns over the kings of the earth.

THESE VERSES ARE SPEAKING OF THE VERY END, RIGHT BEFORE YAHWEH'S RETURN.

Revelation 18:10,17,19,21

[10] IN ONE HOUR IS THY JUDGMENT COME.

[17] IN ONE HOUR...RICHES COME TO NOUGHT.

19 IN ONE HOUR IS SHE MADE DESOLATE |

21 WITH VIOLENCE ZION IS THROWN DOWN.

REVELATION CHAPTER 18:

THIS WHOLE CHAPTER IS SPEAKING ABOUT ZION:

18 And after these things I saw another Messenger come down from heaven, having great power; and the earth was lightened with his righteousness.

2 And he cried mightily with a strong voice, saying, Babylon the great is fallen, is fallen, and is become the habitation of devils, and the hold of every foul spirit, and a cage of every unclean and hateful bird.

3 For all nations have drunk of the wine of the wrath of her fornication, and the kings of the earth have committed fornication with her, and the merchants of the earth are waxed rich through the abundance of her delicacies.

4 And I heard another voice from heaven, saying, Come out of her, my people, that ye be not partakers of her transgressions, and that ye receive not of her plagues.

5 For her transgressions have reached unto heaven, and Yahweh hath remembered her iniquities.

6 Reward her even as she rewarded you, and double unto her double according to her works: in the cup which she hath filled fill to her double.

7 How much she hath glorified herself, and lived deliciously, so much torment and sorrow give her: for she saith in her heart, I sit a queen, and am no widow, and shall see no sorrow.

[8] Therefore shall her plagues come in one day, death, and mourning, and famine; and she shall be utterly burned with fire: for strong is Yahweh who judgeth her.

[9] And the kings of the earth, who have committed fornication and lived deliciously with her, shall bewail her, and lament for her, when they shall see the smoke of her burning,

[10] Standing afar off for the fear of her torment, saying, Alas, alas that great city Babylon, that mighty city! for in one hour is thy judgment come.

[11] And the merchants of the earth shall weep and mourn over her; for no man buyeth their merchandise any more:

[12] The merchandise of gold, and silver, and precious stones, and of pearls, and fine linen, and purple, and silk, and scarlet, and all thyine wood, and all manner vessels of ivory, and all manner vessels of most precious wood, and of brass, and iron, and marble,

[13] And cinnamon, and odors, and ointments, and frankincense, and wine, and oil, and fine flour, and wheat, and beasts, and sheep, and horses, and chariots, and slaves, and souls of men.

[14] And the fruits that thy soul lusted after are departed from thee, and all things which were dainty and goodly are departed from thee, and thou shalt find them no more at all.

[15] The merchants of these things, which were made rich by her, shall stand afar off for the fear of her torment, weeping and wailing,

[16] And saying, Alas, alas that great city, that was clothed in fine linen, and purple, and scarlet, and decked with gold, and precious stones, and pearls!

17 For in one hour so great riches is come to naught. And every shipmaster, and all the company in ships, and sailors, and as many as trade by sea, stood afar off,

18 And cried when they saw the smoke of her burning, saying, What city is like unto this great city!

19 And they cast dust on their heads, and cried, weeping and wailing, saying, Alas, alas that great city, wherein were made rich all that had ships in the sea by reason of her costliness! for in one hour is she made desolate.

20 Rejoice over her, thou heaven, and ye apostles and prophets; for Yahweh hath avenged you on her.

21 And a mighty Messenger took up a stone like a great millstone, and cast it into the sea, saying, Thus with violence shall that great city Babylon be thrown down, and shall be found no more at all.

22 And the voice of harpers, and musicians, and of pipers, and trumpeters, shall be heard no more at all in thee; and no craftsman, of whatsoever craft he be, shall be found any more in thee; and the sound of a millstone shall be heard no more at all in thee;

23 And the light of a candle shall shine no more at all in thee; and the voice of the bridegroom and of the bride shall be heard no more at all in thee: for thy merchants were the great men of the earth; for by thy sorceries were all nations deceived.

24 And in her was found the blood of prophets, and of elect, and of all that were slain upon the earth.

Matthew 23:34-37

34 Wherefore, behold, I send unto you prophets, and wise men, and scribes: and some of them ye shall kill and hang; and some of

them shall ye scourge in your House of Yahweh, and persecute them from city to city:

35 That upon you may come all the righteous blood shed upon the earth, from the blood of righteous Abel unto the blood of Zacharias son of Barachias, whom ye slew between the House of Yahweh and the altar.

36 Verily I say unto you, All these things shall come upon this generation.

37 O Zion, Zion, thou that killest the prophets, and stonest them which are sent unto thee, how often would I have gathered thy children together, even as a hen gathereth her chickens under her wings, and ye would not!

REVELATION CHAPTER 19:

This chapter is self-explanatory and shares details about the end of this world as we know it. Revelation 19:

1 And after these things I heard a great voice of much people in heaven, saying, Halleluyah; Salvation, and honor, and power, unto Yahweh our Mighty One:

2 For true and righteous are his judgments: for He hath judged the great whore, which did corrupt the earth with her fornication, and hath avenged the blood of His servants at her hand.

3 And again they said, Halleluyah. <u>And her smoke rose up for ever and ever.</u>

The Zion we perceive today differs from the Zion that the Messiah once traversed. Furthermore, today's Judaea is a deceptive construct of the Papacy, referred to as Israel. Yahweh is prophesied to reunite all twelve tribes during the 7-Year Peace Plan, with the latter 3 1/2 years constituting the Tribulation period. Salvation will be bestowed upon the 144,000 individuals from these twelve tribes, marking the culmination of divine redemption just prior to the return of Yahweh Messiah. In the climactic event, all the world's armies will converge against Zion, yet it will be the 144,000 who evoke Yahweh's divine presence.

CHAPTER 23
HOUSE NOT TEMPLE

When Constantine started getting rid of the pagan religions and killing a lot of the pagans, he turned their pagan Temples into Christian Churches.

From Wikipedia, the free encyclopedia

The Hebrew noun *hekhal* (Hebrew **היכל**) in Classical Hebrew means "a large building."

Hekhal is used 80 times in the Masoretic Text of the Hebrew Bible. Of these, 70 refer to the House of [Yahweh] the LORD (in Hebrew Bible **בֵּית יְהוָה**: *beit Yahweh*), and the other 10 are references to palaces. There is no reference to any part of the tabernacle using this term in the Hebrew Bible.

"SYNAGOGUE" (SIN-uh-gag): (Sin-a-god- two moon deity names) It is a Greek word. It was used that way in the Septuagint, a Greek translation of the Hebrew Scriptures. This word is traced back to paganism; the word came to refer to the building where Jews assembled for worship. The Greek word synagogue was where pagan worshipers met.

"TEMPLE" (from the Latin word templum) is a structure reserved for religious or spiritual rituals and activities such as prayer and SACRIFICE. In Judaism, the ancient Hebrew texts do not refer to temples. Each of the two ancient temples in Zion was called in the Tanakh, "Beit YAHWEH," which translates literally as "YAHWEH'S HOUSE." Pagans used temples, not the Jews.

"SACRIFICE" = From Sakra, 12 forms of sun-dieties.

Right words: offering or slaughter offering.

PSALMS 52:8 But I am like a green olive tree in the 'House of YAHWEH': I trust in the mercy and faithfulness of YAHWEH forever and ever.

PSALMS 92:13 Those that be planted in the 'House of YAHWEH' shall flourish in the courts of our Sovereign Ruler.

Psalms 23:6 Surely goodness and mercy shall follow me all the days of my life: and I will dwell in the House of Yahweh forever.

PSALMS 134: 1,2

A song of ascents.

[1] Praise Yahweh, all you servants of Yahweh who minister by night in the House of Yahweh.

[2] Lift up your hands in the House and praise Yahweh.

Psalms 122

I was glad when they said to me, "Let us go to the House of Yahweh!"

Our feet have been standing within your gates, O Zion!

Zion, built as a city that is bound firmly together,

to which the tribes go up, the tribes of Yahweh,

as was decreed for Judaea,

to give thanks to the name of Yahweh.

There thrones for judgment were set,

the thrones of the house of David.

Pray for the peace of Zion!

"May they prosper who love you!

Peace be within your walls, and security within your towers!"

For my brethren and companions' sake, I will say, "Peace be within you!"

For the sake of the house of Yahweh our Almighty, I will seek your good.

Matthew 24:1-2

[1] And Immanuel went out, and departed from the House of Yahweh: and his disciples came to him for to shew him the buildings of the House of Yahweh.

[2] And Immanuel said unto them, see ye, not all these things? Verily I say unto you, there shall not be left here one stone upon another, that shall not be thrown down.

Ezekiel 8:16 And he brought me into the inner court of the Yahweh's House, and, behold, at the door of the House of Yahweh, between the porch and the altar, were about five and twenty men, with their backs toward the House of Yahweh, and their faces toward the east; and they worshipped the sun toward the east.

Mark 2:25--26

[25] And he said unto them, have ye never read what David did, when he had need, and was an hungered, he, and they that were with him?

26 How he went into the House of YAHWEH in the days of Abiathar the high priest, and did eat the shewbread, which is not lawful to eat but for the priests, and gave also to them which were with him?

Matthew 21:12,13

12 And Immanuel went into the HOUSE OF YAHWEH, and cast out all them that sold and bought in the House, and overthrew the tables of the moneychangers, and the seats of them that sold doves,

13 And said unto them, It is written, My HOUSE shall be called the House of Prayer; but ye have made it a den of thieves.

Matthew 23:38 Look! Your HOUSE is left to you desolate;

1 Peter 2:5 You also, as living stones, are being built up as a Spiritual House.

1 Corinthians 3:16-17

16 Do you not know that you are a House of Yahweh and that the Spirit of Yahweh dwells in you?

17 If any man defiles the House of Yahweh, Yahweh will destroy him, for the House of Yahweh is righteous, which HOUSE you are.

John 2:19 Immanuel answered and said unto them, destroy this House, and in three days I will raise it up.

Immanuel became the HOUSE for Yahweh's Spirit, thus his Flesh became the House of Yahweh. He was speaking of himself, not the actual building.

Matthew 27:50-51

50 And Immanuel cried out again with a loud voice, and yielded up His spirit.

[51] And behold, the veil of the House [of Yahweh] was torn in two from top to bottom; and the earth shook and the rocks were split.

House of Yahweh worship was done away with when the Messiah died and was resurrected, and that's why the House of Yahweh was destroyed in 70 A.D. So was what we know as Judaism, along with the Levite priesthood and tithing, among other things.

Zechariah 6:12-13

[12] And say to him, 'Thus says Yahweh of hosts, Behold, the man whose name is the Branch: for he shall branch out from his place, and he shall build the House of Yahweh.

[13] It is he who shall build the House of Yahweh and shall bear royal honor, and shall sit and rule on his throne. And there shall be a priest on his throne, and the counsel of peace shall be between them both.

Ephesians 2:21,22

[21] In whom the whole building, being fitted together, growth unto a righteous Temple / HOUSE in Yahweh,

[22] in whom you also are built together into a habitation of Yahweh through the Spirit.

From the beginning of the nineteenth century, the word "temple" began to be used for Jewish houses of worship, almost exclusively by the followers of non-Orthodox movements. It first emerged for Reform Judaism's places of worship in Germany, then spread to other countries, particularly in the United States, as seen in Temple Beth-EL. The House of Yahweh in Zion.

Notice the use of "HOUSES" in the above: "The word 'temple' began to be used for Jewish HOUSES of worship." The same applies to synagogues.

Notice the reference to pagan SYNAGOGUES, which are not considered replacements for the TEMPLE. Both synagogues and temples have pagan origins, obscuring the truth of the HOUSE.

What is referred to as the Temple Mount originated from Gentile terminology. The House of Yahweh was situated on Mount Moriah.

So, Constantine initiated all of this when the world fully succumbed to Satan's influence. As you can see, it is destined to conclude in the same manner it began, with the Pope and Christianity, when Yahweh brings everything to an end."

YOU WILL NOTICE THAT I HAVE INCORPORATED A LOT OF MY OWN WRITTEN POETRY TO ENHANCE MANY OF THE SUBJECTS. I WILL CONCLUDE THIS BOOK BY UTILIZING THEM IN THE SAME TEACHING METHOD.

CHAPTER 24
TEACHING TRUTH BY USING POETRY

WHICH ONE WILL YOU CHOOSE?

Yahweh Messiah verses Jesus Christ,

One is the truth, the other a heist.

Which one should you believe,

To which one should you cleave?

One is for salvation, the other a lie,

Did you search, or did you even try?

It's between two ends, life and death,

Do pick the one that gives life's breath.

One is from inheriting the Father's name,

The other is a pagan name and false claim.

So, if you really are looking for eternal life,

Then, choose the one that will end all strife.

BY Gary W. Stanfield

TRUE SALVATION

There is no salvation for today.

The true Messiah is Yahweh.

That truth will be taught.

Christianity is all for naught.

The 7-Year Peace Plan brings Yahweh's truth,

The Mark of the Beast is sooth.

It's your choice you will choose,

One you win, the other you lose.

The dead that never heard,

The Truth of Yahweh's Word

The Millennium is for them,

All will be taught by Him.

Then there will be no excuse,

When Satan is at last let loose.

To deceive man one last time,

Against humanity, his final crime.

Salvation is with Yahweh's Spirit.

Life is then what you will inherit.

Without having His Spirit infilling,

You will be a lost soul for burning.

This is and has been Satan's world,

In his lies, we have been whirled.

The darker this world seems to get,

Even more, light that is being lit.

By Gary W. Stanfield

In the end, there will be a new heaven and a new earth where Yahweh will live with his Elect.

WHEN THERE WILL BE

When will death be no more?

When will there be no more war,

When will hunger finally be fed,

When will blood no longer be shed?

When there are no more tears,

When there are no more fears,

When there is no more pain,

When riches are not for gain.

When there will be a new birth,

When there will be a new Earth,

When there will be a new day,

When there will be Yahweh!

Then there will be death no more,

Then there will be no more war,

Then, there will be all hunger fed,

Then, there will be no more bloodshed.

By Gary W. Stanfield

YAHWEH'S SPACECRAFT

Yahweh returns in spacecraft, and all the wheat will be caught up in them,

The ones that are saved from Yahweh's wrath, those who had served Him.

Then Yahweh and His Messengers, like birds flying, burn up all the chaff.

People never dreamed that all this will be done with Yahweh's spacecraft.

After this, a great voice of many people in heaven praising Yahweh,

For avenging the blood of His elect while the smoke ascended their way.

They are in spacecraft in heaven above the earth when this praise is done.

Then the elect comes right back to this earth with Yahweh Messiah, the Son.

During His Kingdom, Yahweh teaches all those who never heard His Word,

Between Constantine's time and the 7-year Peace Plan, whose minds were blurred.

That died in Satan's world, infested with our ancestor's pagan lies,

Those who did not believe and turned the truth of Yahweh under a guise.

The whole truth will be taught during the 7-Year Peace Plan; be ready for it.

The miracles and healings once again, just like in the Acts, so do not quit.

Want a spaceship ride, then Yahweh is the Messiah for those who survive?

From that day forward, you will never have to die, forever and eternally alive!

By Gary W. Stanfield

Yahweh left the earth, and through tribulation and death of His elect, this world became Satan's. Then, the next tribulation period and the persecution and death of Yahweh's elect will bring Yahweh back to take back this world from Satan and the power he had given to Satan, the key to the grave and death.

Yahweh's throne is on a spacecraft, Mothership.

I'LL HAVE TWO MORE STUDIES ON SPACRAFT THAT GO DEEPER ABOUT SPACECRAFT IN SCRIPTURES. THOSE WILL HAVE TO WAIT FOR ANOTHER TIME.

Matthew 3:12 Whose fan is in his hand, and he will thoroughly purge his floor, and gather his wheat into the garner; but he will burn up the chaff with unquenchable fire.

Isaiah 31:5 As birds flying, so will Yahweh of hosts defend Zion; defending also he will deliver it; and passing over he will preserve it.

Revelation 19:1-3

[1] And after these things I heard a great voice of much people in heaven, saying, Hallelujah; Salvation, and esteem, and honor, and power, unto Yahweh our Almighty:

2 For true and righteous are His judgments: for He hath judged the great whore (Zion), which did corrupt the earth with her fornication, and hath avenged the blood of his servants at her hand.

3 And again they said, Hallelujah, And her smoke rose (for ever and ever was added)

Youtube.com/watch?t=114s&v=2_n_My84YBw&app=desktop

This guy speaks right along with scriptures about UFOs.

UFO Cover-Up - Robert Dean. Watch from 54:38 to 55:45 on YouTube; from out of the whole video, this part is scripturally true except for the name Jesus that he uses.

https://youtu.be/NvBIuLZrFh0https://youtu.be/NvBIuLZrFh0

An old Yiddish saying says,

"The Messiah you're expecting will never come; the Messiah that's coming you've never expected."

THE 3 HEAVENS:

1. Our Immediate Atmosphere
2. Outer Space (The Sun, Moon, And Stars)
3. The Home of Yahweh

Hebrews 1:14 Seeing then that we have a great High Priest who has passed through the heavens, Yahweh Messiah the Son of Yahweh, let us hold fast our confession.

I can no longer call Yahweh's spacecraft UFOs or unidentified flying objects. The truth is, these are identified by scriptures; the spacecraft we are seeing now are of Satan.

Yahweh kicked Satan out of heaven in a spacecraft to this earth, and he is not allowed to go back.

Spacecraft in scriptures is spoken of as the star, a cloud or clouds, chariots, chariots of fire, white horses, horses, and even angels in a couple places and some other words too.

Acts 1:11. Which also said, Ye men of Galilee, why stand ye gazing up into heaven? This same Yahweh, which is taken up from you into heaven, shall so come in like manner as ye have seen him go into heaven.

A spacecraft took him up, and he will return in a spacecraft.

Isaiah 68:4

4 Sing unto Yahweh, sing praises to His name: extol him that rideth upon the heavens by his name Yahweh, and rejoice before him.

Psalm 104:3 Who layeth the beams of his chambers in the waters: who maketh the clouds his chariot: who walketh upon the wings of the wind:

2 Samuel 22:10-12

10 He bowed the heavens also and came down; and darkness was under his feet.

11 And he rode upon a cherub, and did fly: and he was seen upon the wings of the wind.

12 And he made darkness pavilions round about him, dark waters, and thick clouds of the skies.

Psalm 68:17

17 The Chariots of Yahweh are twenty thousand, even thousands of Messengers: Yahweh is among them, as in Sinai, in the righteous place.

Psalms 18:9-11

9 He bowed the heavens also, and came down: and darkness was under his feet.

10 And He rode upon a cherub, and did fly: yea, He did fly upon the wings of the wind.

11 He made darkness his secret place; his pavilion round about him were dark waters and thick clouds of t

Isaiah 19:1 The burden of Egypt. Behold, Yahweh rideth upon a swift cloud, [spacecraft] and shall come into Egypt: and the idols of Egypt shall be moved at his presence, and the heart of Egypt shall melt in the midst of it.

John 8:23 I am not of this world.

THE CHERUBIMS

When Adam and Eve were kicked out of the Garden of Eden, spacecraft guarded it so no one would enter back.

Genesis 3:24 So he drove out the man; and he placed at the east of the garden of Eden Cherubims, and a flaming sword which turned every way, to keep the way of the tree of life.

2 Samuel 22:10-12

10 He bowed the heavens also, and came down; and darkness was under his feet.

[11] And he rode upon a CHERUB and did fly: and he was seen upon the wings of the wind.

[12] And he made darkness pavilions round about him, dark waters, and thick clouds of the skies.

Cherubims were spacecraft.

NO SUCH THING AS ALIENS:

The first thing Yahweh did in Creation was to make flesh for himself so he could dwell among men. Then, he created the Messengers in his image. Afterward, he created man in his own image, which is why we resemble them, and they resemble us in human form. This is the very reason scriptures state that we could entertain Messengers unaware; they do not have wings as depicted in Christian art. There is no such thing as Aliens, despite what the government wants you to believe. Yahweh and the Messengers were on this earth before we were.

TRANSFIGURATION

<u>Matthew 6:28</u>

Verily I say unto you, there be some standing here, which shall not taste of death, till they see the Son of man coming in his kingdom.

Mark 9:1

And he said unto them, Verily I say unto you, that there be some of them that stand here, which shall not taste of death, till they have seen the kingdom of Yahweh come with power.

Mark 9:2

After six days Immanuel took Peter, James, and John with him and led them up a high mountain, where they were all alone. There he was transfigured before them.

It was Peter, James, and John of whom he was speaking about, as they would not see death till they see him coming into his kingdom.

Luke 9:28-36 tells the same story as Matthew and Mark. In Luke 9:34 it brings out something that Matthew and Mark does not say.

Jeremiah 20:8-9 Whenever I speak, I cry out proclaiming violence and destruction. So, the word of Yahweh has brought me insult and reproach all day long. But if I say, "I will not mention Him or speak any more in His Name," His Word is in my heart like a fire, a fire shut up in my bones. I am weary of holding it in; indeed, I cannot.

THE TRUE SPIRIT INFILLING

People think salvation is for today,

But it is not, and they are led astray.

Away from the truth of the Word.

Preachers keeping the truth all blurred.

Many think they are spirit-filled.

Have you ever seen the crippled healed,

Or a retarded person's mind reversed?

It is not only that, but it even gets worse.

These so-called spirit-filled of today do truly lack,

Once receiving His Spirit, there is no turning back,

This truth people can find in the book of Hebrews,

Chapter 6:4-6 gives you the proof with the clues.

It is impossible, after tasting the heavenly gift,

And Yahweh's judgment on this will be swift.

For they have put the Messiah to open shame,

So, these people's end is in the burning flame.

The Latter Rain of His Spirit is for the 7-Year Peace Plan,

When the whole truth is taught to every man.

This is when the true spirit filled, will have the gifts,

From miracles to healings proved without any ifs.

Satan makes himself look like a messenger of light.

Preachers are called of themselves without sight.

The Spirit will teach the Spirit-filled everything.

They become disciples and ministers of the KING!

By Gary W. Stanfield

ORDER OUT OF CHAOS

There are a few in this world,

Their control of people is hurled.

Aggressively pushing agendas,

And knowing what that does.

The evil of power and greed,

Is on what these people feed.

Taking away every freedom,

To make a one-world kingdom.

Order through chaos is the theme,

All for to hear the people scream.

Knowing that's all people will do,

While evil is tightening the screw.

This is now the age of delusion,

People believe in evolution.

Brainwashed and put to sleep,

No clue as to what they will reap.

This world will worship a man,

It is all in the prophetic plan.

One that wears religious garb,

To the Papacy, this is a barb.

So, wake up, world, it is coming,

The final scenes are drumming.

The 7-Year Peace Plan is at hand,

Will you be one who will withstand?

By Gary W. Stanfield

YOU SHALL SEE

In time, the entire world shall see,

A One World Government there shall be.

Ruled by no one else but the Papacy.

Proven by history and by prophecy.

The Pope cannot wait to take his throne,

When in Zion, he shall be shown.

That is when people will moan and groan,

When this deceitful truth is finally sown.

Then the entire world shall see,

What the Mark of the Beast will be.

Many will think it will set them free,

But this will start the killing spree.

By Gary W. Stanfield

THE END TIME

Yahweh's Spirit infilling must truly be received,

Too many will be without IT and will be deceived.

The spirit filled at that time are going with Him,

Those who are not will see death, which is grim.

During the Peace Plan, the truth to every man, no doubt,

And the Latter Rain of His Spirit is poured out.

After the Tribulation Period, the elect are taken,

When this earth and all those left will be shaken.

Yahweh's wrath is what those on earth will feel,

For all of them, it will be too late for them to kneel.

Then fire shall come down and consume them all,

Later, those who did not listen to Peter and Paul.

The last day on earth turns out not being the last,

Brought right back to this earth, believers will mass.

To reign with Yahweh Messiah in His Kingdom,

The earth will be ruled by Him with all His wisdom.

There are Satan's lies and then Yahweh's truth,

So, study so that you do not end up being uncouth.

The actual heaven for people will be the New Earth,

Yahweh living with His people, who have the new birth.

By Gary W. Stanfield

CHAPTER 25
THE END TIME SYNARIO: ESCHATOLOGY ON THE END TIMES

WORLD WAR 3 – THE BEGINNING TO THE END OF THIS WORLD AS WE KNOW IT.

Daniel 12:4 But thou, O Daniel, shut up the words, and seal the book, even to the time of the end: many shall run to and fro, and knowledge shall be increased.

¹ THE END OF WORLD WAR 3 WILL BRING ABOUT THE PAPACY'S 7-YEAR PEACE PLAN THAT HAPPENS AT THE END OF WW3 TO END IT.

Daniel 9:27 And he shall confirm the covenant with many for one week: (PAPACY'S 7-YEAR PEACE PLAN) and in the midst of the week he shall cause the sacrifice and the oblation to cease, and for the overspreading of abominations he shall make it desolate, even until the consummation, and that determined shall be poured upon the desolate.

THE POPE MOVES HIS THRONE TO ZION, TO THE DOME OF THE ROCK, A FACADE FOR THE TEMPLE OF GOD THAT IS INSIDE THE FACADE. THIS IS THE ABOMINATION OF DESOLATION THAT THE SCRIPTURES SPEAK OF.

2 THESSALONIANS 2:4 Who opposeth and exalteth himself above all that is called A DEITY, or that is worshipped; so that he as A DEITY sitteth in the temple of God, shewing himself that he is A DEITY. It starts with WW3 and ends with the Armageddon War.

THIS IS THE BEGINNING OF THE END AS IT KICKS OFF THE LAST FEW YEARS BEFORE WE MEET OUR MAKER, YAHWEH MESSIAH. WW3 IS THE FIRST GOG AND MAGOG WAR THAT WILL KILL SOME 250 BILLION PEOPLE, 1/3 OF THE WORLD POPULATION. IT WILL BE A LIMITED NUCLEAR WAR.

REVELATION 9:15 And the four Messengers were loosed, which were prepared for an hour, and a day, and a month, and a year, for to slay the third part of men (2 1/2 billion people).

MOSES AND ELIYAH SHOW UP IN ZION AT THE BEGINNING OF THE PAPACY'S 7-YEAR PEACE PLAN THATWILLEND WW3.

Daniel 9:25-27

Know therefore and understand, that from the going forth of the commandment to restore and to build Zion unto the Messiah the King shall be seven weeks, and threescore and two weeks: the street shall be built again, and the wall, even in troublous times. And after threescore and two weeks shall Messiah be cut off, but not for himself: and the people of the king that shall come shall destroy the city and the sanctuary; and the end thereof shall be with a flood, and unto the end of the war desolations are determined. And he shall confirm the covenant with many for one week: and in the midst of the week he shall cause the sacrifice and the oblation to cease, and for the overspreading of abominations he shall make it desolate, even until the consummation, and that determined shall be poured upon the desolate

1 Thessalonians 5:1-3

But of the times and the seasons, brethren, ye have no need that I write unto you. For yourselves know perfectly that the day of Yahweh so cometh as a thief in the night. For when they shall say, Peace and safety; then sudden destruction cometh upon them, as travail upon a woman with child; and they shall not escape.

LET'S SEE WHAT YAHWEH SAYS ABOUT ALL THIS PEACE AND SAFETY STUFF:

Mathew 20:34-35

34 Think not that I am come to send peace on earth: I came not to send peace, but a sword.

35 For I am come to set a man at variance against his father, and the daughter against her mother, and the daughter in law against her mother in law.

Luke 12:49 Have come to bring fire on the earth,

Matthew 10:35 For I am come to set a man at variance against his father, and the daughter against her mother.

Revelations 2:23

And I will kill her children with death; and all the people shall know that I am he which searcheth the reins and hearts: and I will give unto every one of you according to your works.

MOSES AND ELIYAH BRING BACK THE WHOLE TRUTH, AND YAHWEH POURS OUT HIS SPIRIT ON BELIEVERS DURING THAT TIME; THE BOOK OF ACTS WILL BE RELIVED; THE ONES GIVEN SALVATION DURING THIS TIME WILL BE THE ONES THAT WILL NOT TAKE THE MARK OF THE BEAST DURING THE TRIBULATION PERIOD PART OF IT, EVERYONE ELSE WILL. DURING THE TRIBULATION PERIOD, CHRISTIANS WILL KILL THE ELECT OF YAHWEH, AND BECAUSE OF THIS, THE 7 BOWLS WILL BE POURED OUT ON THE WORLD OF PAGAN CHRISTIANS, AND THEY WON'T BE ABLE TO DIE FOR PAYBACK. THEN THEY ARE BURNED

UP IN THE LAKE OF FIRE –There are 2 lakes of Fire. This is the first one; the second lake of Fire is after the second Gog and Magog War, where this earth burns up and melts away AT YAHWEH'S RETURN, THE END FOR THEM TAKING THE MARK TO SAVE THEIR LIVES, BUT YAHWEH WILL TAKE THEIR LIVES IF THEY DO TAKE THE MARK, THE DECISION IS THEIRS.

THIS IS WHEN SALVATION IS GIVEN AGAIN, AND YAHWEH POURS OUT HIS SPIRIT ON THOSE THAT BELIEVE THE WHOLE TRUTH GIVEN AT THAT TIME.

Acts 2:17 "And it shall come to pass in the last days, saith Yahweh, I will pour out of my Spirit upon all flesh, [ALL NATIONS]: and your sons and your daughters shall prophesy, and your young men shall see visions, and your old men shall dream dreams:

"MOSES AND ELIYAH ARE ALIVE DURING THE FIRST 3 1/2 YEARS OF THE 7-YEAR PEACE PLAN AND WHEN THEY TEACH THE WHOLE TRUTH AGAIN TO ALL NATIONS. MIDWAY POINT OF THE 7 YEARS, THE POPE WILL HAVE THEM BOTH KILLED AND WHEN THAT HAPPENS, THAT WILL START THE 3 1/2-YEAR TRIBULATION PERIOD. THIS IS WHEN THE POPE WILL MAKE CHRISTIANITY THE WORLD RELIGION AND HAVE ANYONE THAT DOES NOT COME OVER TO IT KILLED; ONLY YAHWEH'S ELECT WILL NOT GO OVER TO CHRISTIANITY AND WHY THEY WILL BE THE ONES PERSECUTED AND KILLED FOR NOT TAKING THE MARK OF THE BEAST, WHICH WILL BE THE "CROSS." IT WILL BE GIVEN AND ENFORCED BY THE PAPACY.

Daniel 7:25 He [THE POPE] shall speak words against Yahweh and shall wear out the ELECT of the Yahweh and shall think to change the times and the law; and they shall be given into his hand for a time, times, and half a time (3 ½ years).

ONLY THE SPIRIT-FILLED ELECT OF YAHWEH MESSIAH WILL NOT TAKE THE MARK. EVERYONE ELSE WILL TAKE THE MARK. THESE ARE THE ONES THAT YAHWEH WILL KILL AND BURN IN THE LAKE OF FIRE AT HIS COMING.

Matthew 24:9 When they will deliver you up to tribulation and kill you, and you will be hated by all nations for My name's sake.

The Second Ecumenical Council of the Vatican, commonly known as the Second Vatican Council or Vatican II, was the 21st ecumenical council of the Roman Catholic Church.

Date: 11 October 1962 –8 December 1965

EVERY POPE SINCE THE ABOVE COUNCIL HAS PUSHED A WORLD GOVERNMENT. THIS STARTED THE ECUMENICAL MOVEMENT TO UNIFY ALL RELIGIONS AND DENOMINATIONS WITH THE PAPACY AND THE ROMAN CATHOLIC CHURCH. THEY ARE ALL IGNORANT TO THE PURPOSE OF WHAT IS GOING ON.

Revelation 14:9-11

9 And the third Messenger followed them, saying with a loud voice, If any man worship the beast and his image, and receive his mark in his forehead, or in his hand,

10 The same shall drink of the wine of the wrath of Yahweh, which is poured out without mixture into the cup of his indignation; and he shall be tormented with fire and brimstone in the presence of the Messengers, and in the presence of the Lamb:

11 And the smoke of their torment ascendeth up for ever and ever: and they have no rest day nor night, who worship the beast and his image, and whosoever receiveth the mark of his name.

THE ARMAGEDDON WAR STARTS AT THE END OF THE TRIBULATION PERIOD; THE ARMAGEDDON WAR ENDS THE "TRIBULATION PERIOD," AND THE "TIME OF THE GENTILES" ENDS WHEN YAHWEH MESSIAH RETURNS DURING THAT WAR.

ZECHARIAH 14:2 For I will gather all nations against Zion to battle; and the city shall be taken, and the houses rifled, and the women ravished; and half of the city shall go forth into captivity, and the residue of the people shall not be cut off from the city.

ZECHARIAH 13:8 And it shall happen, that in all the land, saith Yahweh, two parts therein shall be cut off and die; but the third shall be left therein.

THE 144,000 SEALED FROM THE 12 TRIBES WILL CALL YAHWEH MESSIAH BACK WHEN ZION IS NEARLY WIPED OUT. THE WORLD ARMIES WILL FIGHT YAHWEH AT HIS COMING WITH SATAN'S HELP, AND THEY ALL WILL BE KILLED.

THE "CATCHING UP": YAHWEH RETURNS IN A SPACECRAFT WITH HIS MESSENGERS TO COLLECT THE ELECT OF YAHWEH. YAHWEH KILLS AND BURNS UP ALL THE WICKED WHO TOOK THE MARK OF THE BEAST—THE CROSS ON THEIR HAND OR FOREHEAD—AFTER HIS ELECT ARE IN THE MOTHER SHIP, PRAISING AND WORSHIPING HIM. HE THEN BRINGS ALL THE ELECT BACK DOWN TO THIS EARTH TO MOUNT ZION TO START HIS MILLENNIAL KINGDOM ON THIS EARTH.

THIS IS WHEN YAHWEH WILL REBUILD THE HOUSE OF YAHWEH. AT THE END OF THE MILLENNIAL KINGDOM IS THE WHITE THRONE JUDGMENT, WHICH IS THE SECOND GOG AND MAGOG WAR. THIS IS THE SECOND LAKE OF FIRE, WHEN ALL THE WICKED BURN UP WITH THIS EARTH AND THE HEAVENS BURN UP.

YAHWEH CREATES A NEW HEAVEN AND A NEW EARTH AND LIVES ON THE NEW EARTH WITH HIS ELECT. NO ONE GOES TO HEAVEN LIKE CHRISTIANITY TEACHES, AND THERE IS NO WAY ANYONE CAN BURN UP IN THE LAKE OF FIRE THAT DOES NOT EVEN EXIST YET UNTIL THE TIMES THAT I HAVE SHOWN YOU.

11:3-6

3 And I will give power unto MY TWO WITNESSES, and they shall PROPHECY a thousand two hundred and threescore days [3 1/2 YEARS] clothed in sackcloth. The first 3 1/2 years of the 7-Year Papacy Peace Plan. The last 3 1/2 years is the Tribulation Period.

4 These are THE TWO OLIVE TREES, and THE TWO CANDLESTICKS standing before YAHWEH of the earth.

5 And if any man will hurt them, fire proceedeth out of their mouth, and devoureth their enemies: and if any man will hurt them, he must in this manner be killed.

6 These have power to shut heaven, that it rain not in the days of THEIR PROPHECY: and have power over waters to turn them to blood, and to smite the earth with all plagues, as often as they will.

THE DEATH OF MOSES AND ELIYAH

7 And when they shall have finished their testimony, the beast [PAPACY] that ascendeth out of the bottomless pit shall make war against them, and shall overcome them, and kill them.

8 And their dead bodies shall lie in the street of the great city, which spiritually is called Sodom and Egypt, where also our MASTER was KILLED.

⁹ And they of the people and kindreds and tongues and nations shall see their dead bodies three days and a half and shall not suffer their dead bodies to be put in graves.

WHAT HAPPENS TO A BODY WITHIN 2 DAYS AFTER DEATH?

24-72 hours (about 3 days) after death, the internal organs decompose. 3-5 days after death, the body starts to bloat, and blood-containing foam leaks from the mouth and nose. Several weeks after death, nails and teeth fall out. 1 month after death, the body starts to liquefy. After 3 1/2 days laying in the street, it will be evident that they are dead, and Yahweh will put life back in their bodies and bring them up to himself within a spacecraft. This is when the 144,000 will realize that Yahweh is their Messiah and worship him. THEY ARE THE ONES WHO CALL YAHWEH BACK.

Chapter 11:10-19

¹⁰ And they that dwell upon the earth shall rejoice over them, and make merry, and shall send gifts one to another; because these two prophets tormented them that dwelt on the earth.

¹¹ And after three days and an half the spirit of life from YAHWEH entered into them, and they stood upon their feet; and great fear fell upon them which saw them.

¹² And they heard a great voice from heaven saying unto them, Come up hither. And they ascended to heaven in a cloud; and their enemies beheld them.

¹³ And the same hour was there a great earthquake, and the tenth part of the city fell, and in the earthquake were slain of men seven thousand: and the remnant were frightened and gave WORSHIP to YAHWEH of heaven.

14 The second woe is past; and, behold, the third woe cometh quickly.

15 And the seventh MESSENGER sounded; and there were great voices in heaven, saying, the kingdoms of this world are become the kingdoms of our YAHWEH, and of his MESSIAH; and he shall reign for ever and ever. VERSE 15 AND 16 ARE SPEAKNG OF HIS MILLENNIAL KINGDOM.

16 And the four and twenty elders, which sat before YAHWEH on their seats, fell upon their faces, and worshiped YAHWEH,

17 Saying, We give thee thanks, O YAHWEH, which art, and wast, and art to come; because thou hast taken to thee thy great power, <u>and hast reigned.</u>

VERSE 17 SHOWS THAT HE ALREADY REIGNED DURING HIS MILLENNIAL KINGDOM

"AND HAST REIGNED" IS PAST TENSE, SO HE HAD ALREADY REIGNED, SO THE WHITE THRONE JUDGEMENT IS NEXT, AND VERSE 18 IS SHOWING THE SECOND GOG AND MAGOG WAR, THE JUDGEMENT WAR, SINCE IT SAYS, "HIS WRATH HAS COME," MEANING FOR HIS JUDGEMENT OF THE WICKED AND SATAN."

18 And the nations were angry, and thy wrath is come, and the time of the dead, that they should be judged, and that thou shouldest give reward unto thy servants the prophets, and to the ELECT, and them that fear thy name, small and great; and shouldest destroy them which destroy the earth.

19 And the HOUSE OF YAHWEH was opened in heaven, and there was seen in HIS HOUSE the Ark of his COVENANT: and there were lightnings, and voices, and thunderings, and an earthquake, and great hail.

THE JUDGEMENT IS ACTUALLY THE WAR BETWEEN YAHWEH AND HIS ELECT AGAINST SATAN AND HIS FOLLOWERS. YAHWEH KILLS THEM ALL WITH THE SECOND LAKE OF FIRE, WHEN ALL THE WICKED BURN UP WITH THIS EARTH AND THE HEAVENS BURN UP. YAHWEH CREATES A NEW HEAVEN AND A NEW EARTH AND LIVES ON THE NEW EARTH WITH HIS ELECT; NO ONE GOES TO HEAVEN.

Daniel 7:13-14

13 I saw in the night visions, and behold, one like the Son of man came with the clouds of heaven, and came to the Ancient of days, and they brought him near before him.

14 And there was given him dominion, and glory, and a kingdom, that all people, nations, and languages, should serve him: his dominion is an everlasting dominion, which shall not pass away, and his kingdom that which shall not be destroyed.

3 THE HAR-MAGEDON WAR WILL END THE 7-YEAR PEACE PLAN. THIS IS WHEN THE PAPACY UNIFIES ALL THE NATIONS OF THE WORLD AS A ONE-WORLD GOVERNMENT TO DESTROY ZION. 144,000 FROM THE 12 TRIBES WILL BE GIVEN SALVATION, AND IT IS THESE WHO WILL CALL YAHWEH BACK. THIS WILL END THE TIMES OF THE GENTILES. THEY REALIZE THAT HE IS THEIR MESSIAH WHEN ZION IS ABOUT TO BE DESTROYED BY THE ARMIES OF THE WORLD.

ZECHARIAH 14:2

For I will gather all nations against ZION to battle; and the city shall be taken, and the houses rifled, and the women ravished; and half of the city shall go forth into captivity, and the residue of the people shall not be cut off from the city.

Revelation 14:6-14

6 And I saw another Messenger fly in the midst of heaven, having the everlasting Word to teach unto them that dwell on the earth, and to every nation, and kindred, and tongue, and people,

7 Saying with a loud voice, Fear Yahweh, and give esteem to him; for the hour of his judgment is come: and worship him that made heaven, and earth, and the sea, and the fountains of waters.

8 And there followed another Messenger, saying, Babylon is fallen, is fallen, that great city, because she made all nations drink of the wine of the wrath of her fornication.

THE ARMAGEDDON WAR IS WHEN ZION FALLS, THAT GREAT CITY.

9 And the third Messenger followed them, saying with a loud voice, If any man worship the beast and his image, and receive his mark in his forehead, or in his hand,

DURING TRIBULATION.

10 The same shall drink of the wine of the wrath of Yahweh, which is poured out without mixture into the cup of his indignation; and he shall be tormented with fire and brimstone in the presence of the Messengers, and in the presence of the Lamb:

11 And the smoke of their torment ascendeth up for ever and ever: and they have no rest day nor night, who worship the beast and his image, and whosoever receiveth the mark of his name. YAHWEH MESSIAH'S RETURN.

12 Here is the patience of the Elect: here are they that keep the commandments of Yahweh, and the faith of Immanuel.

SPIRIT INFILLING

13 And I heard a voice from heaven saying unto me, Write, Blessed are the dead which die in Yahweh from henceforth: Yea, saith the Spirit, that they may rest from their labours; and their works do follow them.

14 And I looked, and behold a white cloud, and upon the cloud one sat like unto the Son of man, having on his head a golden crown, and in his hand a sharp sickle.

THE RETURN OF YAHWEH MESSIAH. HE IS RETURNING IN SPACECRAFT ALONG WITH ALL HIS MESSENGERS THAT HE SENDS OUT TO COLLECT ALL THE ELECT AT THAT TIME. HE THEN POURS HIS WRATH OUT ON THE WORLD OF UNBELIEVERS, WHO ARE THE ONLY ONES LEFT AFTER THE ELECT ARE ALL TAKEN UP INTO ALL THE SPACECRAFT, AND THEY ARE TAKEN TO THE MOTHER-SHIP WHERE YAHWEH'S THRONE IS. THEY ARE WITH HIM IN HIS THRONE ROOM ABOVE THE EARTH, PRAISING YAHWEH. THIS IS THE GREAT GULF SPOKEN OF IN THE STORY OF LAZARUS AND THE RICH MAN. ALL THE PEOPLE LEFT ON THE EARTH WILL BE KILLED ALONG WITH ALL THE ARMIES AND BURNED UP, NEVER TO EXIST AGAIN. This is the first lake of fire.

Zephaniah 3:8

"Therefore wait ye upon me, saith Yahweh, until the day that I rise up to the prey: for my determination is to gather the nations, that I may assemble the kingdoms, to pour upon them mine indignation, even all my fierce anger: for all the earth shall be devoured with the fire of my jealousy"

YAHWEH THEN BRINGS HIS ELECT WITH HIM BACK TO THIS EARTH TO MOUNT ZION TO RULE WITH HIM DURING HIS MILLENNIAL KINGDOM OF A THOUSAND YEARS. HE RAISES ALL THOSE THAT HAD DIED WITHOUT EVER HEARING THE TRUTH, WHICH GOES ALL THE WAY BACK TO CONSTANTINE, AND YAHWEH WILL TEACH THESE PEOPLE HIMSELF. ANYONE THAT NEVER HEARD THE WHOLE TRUTH FOR SALVATION CANNOT BE JUDGED UNLESS THEY HAVE HEARD IT AND BELIEVED IT FOR SALVATION OR NOT TO BELIEVE IT AND BE FOREVER LOST. YOU MUST BE SPIRIT-FILLED TO BE GIVEN SALVATION; THIS IS WHEN A GENTILE OR JEW BECOMES A JUDAEAN.

WHITE THRONE JUDGEMENT HAPPENS AT THE END OF YAHWEH MESSIAH'S MILLENNIAL KINGDOM. THE JUDGEMENT IS WHEN THE WICKED ARE BURNED UP WITH THIS EARTH. THEN YAHWEH CREATES A NEW HEAVEN AND NEW EARTH AND LIVES WITH HIS ELECT ON THE NEW EARTH. YAHWEH LIVES WITH HIS ELECT ON THE NEW EARTH, NOT IN HEAVEN.

Romans 11:25 For I would not, brethren, that ye should be ignorant of this mystery, lest ye should be wise in your own conceits; that blindness in part is happened to Judaea, until the fulness of the Gentiles be come in.

YAHWEH KILLS AND BURNS UP ALL THE WICKED THAT TOOK THE MARK AFTER HIS ELECT ARE IN THE MOTHERSHIP, PRAISING AND WORSHIPING HIM. HE THEN BRINGS ALL THE

ELECT RIGHT BACK DOWN TO THIS EARTH TO MOUNT ZION TO START HIS MILLENNIAL KINGDOM ON THIS EARTH. THIS IS WHEN YAHWEH WILL REBUILD THE HOUSE OF YAHWEH.

AT THE END OF THE MILLENNIAL KINGDOM IS THE WHITE THRONE JUDGMENT, WHICH IS THE SECOND GOG AND MAGOG WAR. THIS IS ALSO THE 2ND LAKE OF FIRE WHEN ALL THE WICKED BURN UP WITH THIS EARTH AND THE HEAVENS BURN UP.

2 PETER 3;10

But the day of Yahweh will come as a thief in the night; in the which the heavens shall pass away with a great noise, and the elements shall melt with fervent heat, the earth also and the works that are therein shall be burned up.

1. DEVIL = SATAN
2. BEAST = PAPACY GOVERNMENT / REPRESENTED BY THE BLACK POPE
3. FALSE PROPHET - ANTI-MESSIAH – MAN OF TRANSGRESSIONS – THE WHITE POPE IS OVER CHRISTIANITY THAT WILL ABSORB ALL PAGAN RELIGIONS OF THE WORLD. BOTH POPES ARE THE IMAGE OF THE BEAST/PAPACY.

ZECHARIAH 14:2

For I will gather all nations against Zion to battle; and the city shall be taken, and the houses rifled, and the women ravished; and half of the city shall go forth into captivity, and the residue of the people shall not be cut off from the city.

Zechariah 14:16-19

16 And it shall come to pass, that every one that is left of all the nations which came against Zion shall even go up from year to year to worship the King of hosts, and to keep the feast of tabernacles.

17 And it shall be, that whoso will not come up of all the families of the earth unto Zion to worship the King of hosts, even upon them shall be no rain.

18 And if the family of Egypt go not up, and come not, that have no rain; there shall be the plague, wherewith Yahweh will smite the heathen that come not up to keep the feast of tabernacles.

19 This shall be the punishment of Egypt, and the punishment of all nations that come not up to keep the feast of the tabernacle.

CHAPTER 26
THE DESTRUCTION OF ZION

Revelation 14:8

[8] And there followed another Messenger, saying, Babylon is fallen, is fallen, that great city, because she made all nations drink of the wine of the wrath of her fornication. The city of Zion is the one fallen.

Revelation 18:10,17,19,21

[10] IN ONE HOUR THY/ ZION'S JUDGMENT COME.

[17] IN ONE HOUR...ZION'S RICHES COME TO NOUGHT.

[19] IN ONE HOUR IS SHE/ZION MADE DESOLATE|

[21] With violence Zion is thrown down.

Revelation17:16,17

[16] And the ten horns which thou sawest upon the beast, these shall hate the whore, and shall make her desolate and naked, and shall eat her flesh, and burn her with fire.

[17] For Yahweh hath put in their hearts to fulfil his will, and to agree, and give their kingdom unto the beast/Papacy, until the words of Yahweh shall be fulfilled.

REVELATION 19:2

[2] For true and righteous are his judgments: for he hath judged the great whore, which did corrupt the earth with her fornication, and hath avenged the blood of his servants at her hand.

Revelation chapter 18

1 And after these things I saw another Messenger come down from heaven, having great power; and the earth was lightened with his righteousness.

2 And he cried mightily with a strong voice, saying, Babylon the great is fallen, is fallen, and is become the habitation of devils, and the hold of every foul spirit, and a cage of every unclean and hateful bird.

3 For all nations have drunk of the wine of the wrath of her fornication, and the kings of the earth have committed fornication with her, and the merchants of the earth are waxed rich through the abundance of her delicacies.

4 And I heard another voice from heaven, saying, Come out of her, my people, that ye be not partakers of her transgressions, and that ye receive not of her plagues.

5 For her transgressions have reached unto heaven, and God hath remembered her iniquities.

6 Reward her even as she rewarded you, and double unto her double according to her works: in the cup which she hath filled fill to her double.

7 How much she hath glorified herself, and lived deliciously, so much torment and sorrow give her: for she saith in her heart, I sit a queen, and am no widow, and shall see no sorrow.

8 Therefore shall her plagues come in one day, death, and mourning, and famine; and she shall be utterly burned with fire: for strong *is* Yahweh who judgeth her.

9 And the kings of the earth, who have committed fornication and lived deliciously with her, shall bewail her, and lament for her, when they shall see the smoke of her burning,

10 Standing afar off for the fear of her torment, saying, Alas, alas, that great city Babylon, that mighty city! for in one hour is thy judgment come.

11 And the merchants of the earth shall weep and mourn over her; for no man buyeth their merchandise any more:

12 The merchandise of gold, and silver, and precious stones, and of pearls, and fine linen, and purple, and silk, and scarlet, and all thyine wood, and all manner vessels of ivory, and all manner vessels of most precious wood, and of brass, and iron, and marble,

13 And cinnamon, and odours, and ointments, and frankincense, and wine, and oil, and fine flour, and wheat, and beasts, and sheep, and horses, and chariots, and slaves, and souls of men.

14 And the fruits that thy soul lusted after are departed from thee, and all things which were dainty and goodly are departed from thee, and thou shalt find them no more at all.

15 The merchants of these things, which were made rich by her, shall stand afar off for the fear of her torment, weeping and wailing,

16 And saying, Alas, alas, that great city, that was clothed in fine linen, and purple, and scarlet, and decked with gold, and precious stones, and pearls!

17 For in one hour so great riches is come to nought. And every shipmaster, and all the company in ships, and sailors, and as many as trade by sea, stood afar off,

¹⁸ And cried when they saw the smoke of her burning, saying, What *city is* like unto this great city!

¹⁹ And they cast dust on their heads, and cried, weeping and wailing, saying, Alas, alas, that great city, wherein were made rich all that had ships in the sea by reason of her costliness! for in one hour is she made desolate.

²⁰ Rejoice over her, *thou* heaven, and *ye righteous* apostles and prophets; for Yahweh hath avenged you on her.

²¹ And a mighty Messenger took up a stone like a great millstone, and cast *it* into the sea, saying, Thus with violence shall that great city Babylon be thrown down, and shall be found no more at all.

²² And the voice of harpers, and musicians, and of pipers, and trumpeters, shall be heard no more at all in thee; and no craftsman, of whatsoever craft *he be*, shall be found any more in thee; and the sound of a millstone shall be heard no more at all in thee;

²³ And the light of a candle shall shine no more at all in thee; and the voice of the bridegroom and of the bride shall be heard no more at all in thee: for thy merchants were the great men of the earth; for by thy sorceries were all nations deceived.

²⁴ And in her was found the blood of prophets, and of saints/elect, and of all that were slain upon the earth.

All humanity must hear the whole truth, and those who have died who never did must also, without knowing the whole truth, no one can be judged since they never received the opportunity for salvation. Yahweh has made a way for the living and the dead to hear the whole truth because all humanity will be judged, except for the Elect, who were given salvation before that time at the White Throne Judgement.

CHAPTER 27
SOME PAGAN WORDS PUT INTO THE SCRIPTURES

"LUCIFER"

Since the fourth Century, the word Lucifer is sometimes used in Christian theology to refer to Satan; LUCIFER IS A PAGAN DEITY NAME. In the 4th century, Constantine had 50 copies of his propagandized scriptures in Greek.

The actual name, "Lucifer," goes back to the Greeks before the Romans. Socrates and Plato talk about this "deity of light," surprisingly, not in the context of Eos (deity of Dawn), but -- as a morning star -- to place side by side with the sun (Helios) and Hermes. This information can be found in Plato's Timaeus and in Edith Hamilton's Mythology." Constantine in his version would have used the word "εωσφόρος" eosfóros - 'dawn- bringer'

Used in Isaiah 14.12, "How art thou fallen from heaven, O Lucifer (HALAL), son of the morning! How art thou cut down to the ground, which didst weaken the nations! "Comes from Jerome's Latin Vulgate, where it originated. Jerome put Constantine's scriptures into Latin, and "LUCIFER," a pagan deity, is a Latin name for the planet Venus. Meaning "the morning star."

In the year 326, Constantine sent his mother Helena to Jerusalem/Zion to discover the spot that he had foreseen in a vision as the place of Immanuel's Resurrection. This was the site of the temple of Venus on the western side of Jerusalem/Zion. He ordered the temple torn down and a church constructed on the site. This is called the church of the "Holy" Sepulcher to this day. What had been this Temple of Venus? When the Romans finally conquered Jerusalem/Zion in 135 A.D., as an insult to the Jews, they built a Temple of Venus over a monument to a monument to a Jewish freedom fighter named John Hyrcanus.

The only place Lucifer is mentioned in scripture and now is replaced with "morning star." It is the worship of Satan. The Romans even built a temple to Venus in Jerusalem/Zion. The temple of Venus is on the western side of Zion. Constantine ordered the temple torn down and a church constructed on the site. This is called the church of the "Holy" Sepulcher to this day.

The Hebrew phrase is "Heylel ben Shakar" Jerome used the word Lucifer for Heylel. Constantine put the Hebrew into the Greek, not Jerome.

The only place Lucifer is mentioned in scripture now is replaced with "morning star." It is the worship of Satan.

What had been this Temple of Venus? When the Romans finally conquered Jerusalem in 135 A.D., as an insult to the Jews, they built a Temple of Venus over a monument to a Jewish freedom fighter named John Hyrcanus.

The actual name, "Lucifer," goes back to the Greeks before the Romans. Socrates and Plato talk about this "deity of light"; surprisingly, not in the context of Eos (g/d of Dawn), but -- as a morning star -- juxtaposed with the sun (Helios) and Hermes. This information can be found in Plato's Timaeus (38e) and in Edith Hamilton's Mythology."

"ESTHER"

Rabbi Shmuel: Look, the Book of Esther is a pagan book. Queen Esther is named after the fertility deity Ishtar, Mordechai is named after a war god, Marduk, and Haman is obviously a stand-in for the deity of death, defeated by Marduk. Vashti possibly might refer to a Persian deity named Mashti. Some don't believe the book of Esther should even be added to the other books because it's purely a secular historical book.

"GENTILE"

Put Pagan or Pagans where Gentile or Gentiles are in the scriptures. All Gentile countries were Pagan countries.

THE PAGAN WORD "TRINITY"

"TRINITY" comes from paganism. The Trinity doctrine did not enter Christianity until the 300's. *"The trinity got its start in Ancient Babylon with Nimrod – Tammuz - and Semiramis.*

However, the indebtedness of Christian theological theory to ancient Egyptian dogma is nowhere more striking than in the doctrine of the Trinity. The very terms used of it by Christian theologians meet us again in the inscriptions and papyri of Egypt.

Originally the Trinity was a triad like those we find in Babylonian mythology. The triad consisted of a divine father, wife, and son. The father became the son and the son the father through all time, and of both alike, the mother was but another form."

Most of Christianity teaches a Trinity doctrine that the trinity is 3 persons, the Father, Son, and Spirit. In that case, there should also be 3 thrones, yet the scriptures teach that there is only one throne.

Psalms 47:8 Yahweh reigns over the nations; Yahweh sits on his righteous throne.

Isaiah 6:1 In the year that King Uzziah died I saw Yahweh sitting upon a throne, high and lifted up; and the train of his robe filled the House.

Revelation 4:2 At once I was in the Spirit, and behold, a throne stood in heaven, with one seated on the throne.

Revelation 3:21 The one who conquers, I will grant him to sit with me on my throne, as I also conquered and sat down with my Father on his throne.

Psalms 11:4 Yahweh is in his righteous House; Yahweh's throne is in heaven; his eyes see; his eyelids test the children of man.

Revelation 22:1 Then the Messenger showed me the river of the water of life, bright as crystal, flowing from the throne of Yahweh and of the Lamb.

<u>Just One Throne.</u>

"TRINITY"

Nimrod is the one who started pagan religions, and the Trinity belief goes back to him. He turned his back on Yahweh and became the first False Messiah, Sol the Sun, who went by many different names after the Tower of Babel, from the many cultures that came from Yahweh changing their languages and dispersing them, starting new cultures and beliefs. The Trinity doctrine did not enter Christianity until the 300's. Ancient religions had triple deities:

Wicca triple goddesses Maiden, Mother, and Crone. Greeks Zeus, Poseidon, and Hades

Is there a Trinity in Greek mythology?

The Greek trinity and the distribution of the three kingdoms of the Earth: Zeus God (Heaven), Poseidon (Seas and oceans), and Hades (Underworld). Theos (minor gods) are the children of this trinity.

Romans Jupiter, Neptune, and Pluto.

Hindu's Brahma, Vishnu, and Shiva.Norse Odin, Vili, and Ve.

Toaist

The first Pure One is universal or heavenly chi. The second Pure One is human plane chi, and the third Pure One is earth chi. Worship for the Taoist Trinity dates back to the 4th century.

Egyptians Isis, Horus, and Seth. -- IHS is a popular Latinized monogram acronym from the Roman 3rd Century

Trinity: The oldest creed that Egypt had known for thousands of years was based on the Holy Trinity, the Father God Osiris, the Mother Goddess Isis, and the Son Horus, whom Isis bore without defiling herself.

Horus is the son of Osiris and Isis, the divine child of the holy family triad. He is one of many gods associated with the falcon. His name means "he who is above" and "he who is distant."

THE REAL TRUTH ABOUT "GRACE"

GRACE IS USED 150 TIMES IN THE SCRIPTURES.

All you hear today are preachers teaching the people that they are under GRACE, but GRACE is a pagan deity name. Let us see what words GRACE replaced in some of the verses in the scriptures.

Psalms 103:4 He redeems your life from the pit, he surrounds you with grace / LOVE and compassion,

Colossians 3:16 Let the Word of Christ / Yahweh dwell in you richly in all wisdom; teaching and admonishing one another in psalms and songs and spiritual songs, singing with grace / PRAISE in your hearts to Yahweh.

Hebrews 4:16 Let us then with confidence draw near to the throne of grace / YAHWEH, that we may receive mercy and find grace / YAHWEH to help in time of need.

2 Timothy 2:1 Thou therefore, my son, be strong in the grace / FAITH that is in Yahweh.

Romans 1:5 By whom we have received grace / the SPIRIT and apostleship, for obedience to the faith among all nations, for His name:

1 Corinthians 15:10 But by the grace / SPIRIT of Yahweh I am what I am: and His grace / SPIRIT which *was bestowed* upon me was not in vain; but I labored more abundantly than they all: yet not I, but the grace / SPIRIT of Yahweh which was with me.

Acts 15:11 But we believe that we shall be saved through the grace / SPIRIT of Yahweh, in like manner as they.

2 Corinthians 12:9 And he said unto me, my grace /SPIRIT is sufficient for thee: for my strength is made perfect in weakness. Most gladly therefore will I glory / PRAISE in my infirmities, that the power of Christ / YAHWEH may rest upon me.

John 1:14 And the Word became flesh and dwelt among us, and we have seen his righteousness, esteemed as of the only Son from the Father, full of grace / SPIRIT and truth.

Acts 4:33 And with great power the apostles were giving their testimony to the resurrection of Yahweh Messiah, and great [WAS THE] grace / SPIRIT [THAT] was upon them all.

Acts 6:8 And Stephen, full of grace / SPIRIT and power, was doing great wonders and signs among the people.

Acts 11:23 Who, when he came, and had seen the grace / POWER of Yahweh, was glad, and exhorted them all, that with purpose of heart they would cleave unto Yahweh.

Acts 20:32 And now I commend you to Yahweh and to the Word of his grace / SPIRIT, which is able to build you up and to give you the inheritance among all those who are called out.

Romans 1:5 By whom we have received grace / FAVOR and apostleship, for obedience to the faith among all nations, for his name:

Romans 3:24 Being justified freely by his grace / SPIRIT through the redemption that is in Messiah Yahweh:

Galatians 3 Grace / PEACE be to you and peace from Yahweh the Father, and from our Master Yahweh Messiah,

Ephesians 2:5,8

5 Even when we were dead in transgressions, hath quickened us together with Christ / Yahweh Messiah, (by grace/ THE SPIRIT ye are saved;)

6 And hath raised us up together, and made us sit together in heavenly places in Messiah Yahweh:

7 That in the ages to come he might shew the exceeding riches of his grace / MERCIES in his kindness toward us through Messiah Yahweh.

8 For by grace / HIS SPIRIT are ye saved through faith; and that not of yourselves: it is the gift of Yahweh:

Acts 20:24 But I hold not my life of any account as dear unto myself, so that I may accomplish my course, and the ministry which I received from the Lord / YAHWEH, to testify the Word of the grace / SPIRIT of God / Yahweh.

1 Corinthians 15:10 But by the grace / SPIRIT of Yahweh I am what I am: and His grace / SPIRIT which was bestowed upon me was not in vain; but I labored more abundantly than they all: yet not I, but the grace / SPIRIT of God / Yahweh which was with me.

Ephesians 4:7 But unto every one of us is given grace / FAITH according to the measure of the gift of Christ / Yahweh.

Acts 15:11 But we believe that we shall be saved through the grace/SPIRIT of Yahweh, in like manner as they.

2 Peter 1:2 Grace / BLESSING and peace be yours in abundance through the knowledge of Yahweh and of Yahweh our Master.

2 Corinthians 9:8 And Yahweh is able to make all grace / BOUNTIFULNESS abound toward you; that ye, always having all sufficiency in all things, may abound to every good work:

Zechariah 12: And I will pour upon the house of David, and upon the inhabitants of Zion, the spirit of grace / FORGIVENESS and of supplications: and they shall look upon me whom they have pierced, and they shall mourn for him, as one mourneth for his only son, and shall be in bitterness for him, as one that is in bitterness for his firstborn.

Romans 1:7 To all that be in Rome, beloved of God / Yahweh, called to be saints / elect: Grace / PEACE to you and peace from God / Yahweh our Father, and the Lord Jesus Christ / Master Yahweh Messiah

The following verses where GRACE was put is where PEACE goes: 1 Corinthians 1:3; Corinthians 1:2; Galatians 1:3; Philippians 1:2; Colossians 1:2; 1 Thessalonians 1:1; 2 Thessalonians 1:2; 1 Timothy 1:2; 2; Timothy 1:2; Titus 1:4.

This is Grace in Greek Mythology. The Trinity female deity of Joy, Charm, and Beauty!

"Grace" comes from the Greek word "charis" and the Latin word "gratia." "Charis" was a Greek deity, the wife of Vulcan. From the female deity "Charis" comes the Greek "Charities," three female deities, daughters of "Helios," the Greek/Roman high Sun-deity.

The name Gratus is of Latin origin. The meaning of Gratus is "grace."

The Catholics teach this: "Hail (Mary), full of GRACE, the Lord is with thee" (Luke 1:28)

Below is an example of how the verse should be read.

[28] And the Messenger came in unto her, and said, Hail, thou that art highly favoured, Yahweh is with thee: blessed art thou among women.

CHAPTER 28
IN THE NAME, NOT NAMES OF THE FATHER, SON, AND SPIRIT

1 John 5:7

For there are three that bear record in heaven, the Father, the Word, and the Spirit: and these three are one.

This above verse goes right along with Matthew 28:19 above this verse.

It does not promote a TRINITY; Christianity did that.

Yahweh the Father is Spirit, so that takes care of Father and Spirit; the SON / FLESH / WORD, Yahweh put Himself into the FLESH fully. The name people were baptized into was YAHWEH. Father, Son, and Spirit are offices of Yahweh; the name never changes, only the office. Yahweh is not a Trinity, but ONE. SELF-SAME-SPIRIT, SELF-SAME HIMSELF. Thus, you have YAHWEH MESSIAH, YAHWEH the FATHER, which is SPIRIT in the FLESH. Yahweh is ONE, not a TRINITY. He put on the FLESH to dwell among men and to become the offered Lamb. He revealed Himself through the FLESH and the SPIRIT.

John 14:16-21 - In these verses, he is saying that he is the Spirit.

16 And I will pray the Father, and he shall give you another Comforter, that he may abide with you forever;

¹⁷ Even the Spirit of truth; whom the world cannot receive, because it seeth him not, neither knoweth him: but ye know him; for he dwelleth with you and shall be in you.

¹⁸ I will not leave you comfortless: I will come to you. [HE IS SAYING HERE THAT HE IS THE SPIRIT]

¹⁹ Yet a little while, and the world seeth me no more; but ye see me: because I live, ye shall live also.

²⁰ At that day ye shall know that I am in my Father, and ye in me, and I in you.

²¹ He that hath my commandments, and keepeth them, he it is that loveth Me: and he that loveth Me shall be loved of my Father, and I will love him, and WILL MANIFEST MYSELF TO HIM.

Isaiah 9:6 For unto us a child is born, unto us a son is given: and the government shall be upon his shoulder: and his name shall be called Wonderful, Counsellor, The Mighty One, THE EVERLASTING FATHER, The King of Peace.

Isaiah 9:6 For unto us a child is born, unto us a son is given: and the government shall be upon his shoulder: and his name shall be called Wonderful, Counsellor, The Mighty One, THE EVERLASTING FATHER, The King of Peace.

Matthew 28:19 Go ye therefore and teach all nations, baptizing them in the NAME of the Father, and of the Son, and of the Spirit.

Deuteronomy 6:4 "Hear, O Israel: Yahweh our Mighty One *is* one Yahweh:"

¹ YAHWEH, THE FATHER, IS SPIRIT.

2 THE SON IS THE FLESH WITH THE FATHER, WHO IS SPIRIT IN THE FLESH FULLY, YAHWEH MESSIAH / THE FATHER IN THE FLESH FULLY.

3 THROUGH THE SELF-SAME SPIRIT, HIMSELF; YAHWEH IS ONE, NOT A TRINITY.

5 FATHER, SON, AND SPIRIT ARE OFFICES OF YAHWEH

6 BE BAPTIZED IN THE NAME, NOT NAMES OF THE FATHER, SON, AND SPIRIT, THAT NAME WAS YAHWEH THAT THE ELECT WERE BAPTIZED IN AND NO OTHER.

CHAPTER 29
YAHWEH'S SEAL

John 3:33,34

³³ He that hath received his testimony hath set to his seal that Yahweh is true.

³⁴ For he whom Yahweh hath sent speaketh the words of Yahweh: for Yahweh giveth not the Spirit by measure unto him.

John 6:27 Labor not for the meat which perisheth, but for that meat which endureth unto everlasting life, which the Son of man shall give unto you: for him hath Yahweh the Father Sealed

Revelation 7:2-4

² And I saw another Messenger ascending from the east, having the seal of the living Yahweh: and he cried with a loud voice to the four Messengers, to whom it was given to hurt the earth and the sea

³ Saying, hurt not the earth, neither the sea, nor the trees, till we have sealed the servants of Yahweh in their forehead

⁴ And I heard the number of them which were sealed: and there were sealed a hundred and forty and four thousands of all the tribes of the children of Israel.

Revelation 5:1-6

¹ And I saw in the right hand of him that sat on the throne a book written within and on the backside, sealed with seven seals.

2 And I saw a strong Messenger proclaiming with a loud voice, Who is worthy to open the book, and to loose the seals thereof?

3 And no man in heaven, nor in earth, neither under the earth, was able to open the book, neither to look thereon

4 And I wept much, because no man was found worthy to open and to read the book, neither to look thereon

5 And one of the elders saith unto me, Weep not: behold, the Lion of the tribe of Juda, the Root of David, hath prevailed to open the book, and to loose the seven seals thereof.

6 And I beheld, and, lo, in the midst of the throne and of the four beasts, and in the midst of the elders, stood a Lamb as it had been slain, having seven horns and seven eyes, which are the seven Spirits of Yahweh sent forth into all the earth

2 Corinthians 1:21-22

21 Now he which established us with you in the Messiah, and hath anointed us, is Yahweh

22 Who hath also sealed us, and given the earnest of the Spirit in our hearts

Ephesians 4:30 And grieve not the Spirit of Yahweh, whereby ye are sealed unto the day of redemption

Romans 8:14-16

14 So then they that are in the flesh cannot please Yahweh.

15 For ye have not received the spirit of bondage again to fear; but ye have received the Spirit of adoption, whereby we cry, Abba, Father.

[16] The Spirit itself beareth witness with our Spirit, that we are the children of Yahweh.

Romans 8:8-9

[8] So then they that are in the flesh cannot please Yahweh

[9] But ye are not in the flesh, but in the Spirit, if so be that the Spirit of Yahweh dwell in you. Now if any man has not the Spirit of Yahweh, he is none of his.

Romans 8:11 But if the Spirit of Him that raised up Immanuel from the dead dwell in you, he that raised up the Messiah from the dead shall also quicken your mortal bodies by his Spirit that dwelleth in you

2 Corinthians 13:5 Examine yourselves, whether ye be in the faith; prove your own selves. Know ye not your own selves, how that Yahweh the Messiah is in you, except ye be reprobates

Yahweh's Spirit is HIS seal

Some teach the Sabbath is the Seal, but if that were the case, the whole 10 commandments would have to be. If you break one, you break them all.

Ezekiel 36:27 And I will put my Spirit within you, and cause you to walk in my statutes, and ye shall keep my judgments, and do them.

1 Corinthians 15:24 Then cometh the end, when he shall have delivered up the kingdom to Yahweh, even the Father; when he shall have put down all rule and all authority and power.

NOTE: Yahweh will no longer be spoken of as the Father and or the Son. He will be known then as the Father only in the Flesh.

A LITTLE RAT POISON MIXED WITH THE GOOD STUFF STILL KILLS THE RAT.

Revelation 18:4 And I heard another voice from heaven, saying, Come out of her (Zion with the Babylonian religious system as world religion), my people, that ye be not partakers of her transgressions, and that ye receive not of her plagues.

Matthew 22:14

14 For many are called, but few are chosen. (For his Spirit infilling which gives salvation.)

Isaiah 24:6 Therefore hath the curse devoured the earth, and they that dwell therein are desolate: therefore the inhabitants of the earth are burned, and few men left.

Christianity was created to put people into the Lake of Fire, not to save them from it.

I do not believe that humanity will know all the lies that were perpetuated into the scriptures until Moses and Eliyah bring back the whole truth once again.

YAHWEH MESSIAH

Immanuel was born through the flesh of man.

Born of a virgin through the Father's plan.

He died on an Olive tree as the offered Lamb.

We know now He is the great "I Am."

Who had died for the transgressions of man.

Yahweh Messiah, scriptures prove it's He.

He says, there is no Savior besides Me.

He's the flesh of the Father, can't you see?

He is the only one that can set you free.

If only you would believe that He is He.

By Gary W. Stanfield

CHAPTER 30
YAHWEH MESSIAH KILLED

1. THE LAST DAY MESSAGE THAT WILL TURN THE WORLD UPSIDE DOWN ONE LAST TIME.

John 1:1 IN THE BEGINNING WAS THE WORD, and THE WORD WAS WITH YAHWEH, AND THE WORD WAS YAHWEH.

1 Timothy 3:16 And without controversy great is the mystery of righteousness: YAHWEH WAS MANIFEST IN THE FLESH, justified in the Spirit, seen of Messengers, preached/taught unto the Gentiles, believed on in the world, received up into heaven.

Colossians 1:15-17,19

15 WHO IS THE IMAGE OF THE INVISIBLE YAHWEH, the first born of all creation;

16 FOR IN HIM WERE ALL THINGS CREATED, IN THE HEAVENS AND UPON THE EARTH, THINGS VISIBLE, INVISIBLE, WHITHER THRONES OR DOMINIONS OR PRINCIPALITIES OR POWERS; ALL THINGS HAVE BEEN CREATED THROUGH HIM, AND TO HIM.

17 AND HE IS BEFORE ALL THINGS, AND IN HIM ALL THINGS CONSIST.

19 FOR IT WAS THE GOOD PLEASURE OF THE FATHER THAT IN HIM SHOULD ALL THE FULNESS DWELL;

Colossians 2:9 FOR IN HIM DWELLETH ALL THE FULNESS OF YAHWEH BODILY.

2 John 1:7 For MANY DECEIVERS ARE ENTERED INTO THE WORLD, WHO CONFESS NOT THAT YAHWEH IS COME IN THE FLESH. THIS IS A DECEIVER AN ANTI-MESSIAH.

Acts 18:28 For he mightily convinced the Jews, and that publicly, SHOWING BY THE SCRIPTURES THAT YAWHEH WAS THE MESSIAH.

Luke 2:11 For unto you is born this day in the city of David a Savior, WHICH IS MESSIAH YAHWEH.

Matthew 16:20 Then he ordered his disciples not to tell anyone that he was the Messiah.

Acts 17:3 Opening and alleging, that the Messiah must needs have suffered, and risen again from the dead; and THAT THIS IMMANUEL, WHOM I PREACH/TEACH UNTO YOU, IS YAHWEH.

1 Corinthians 1:23 But WE PREACH YAHWEH IMPALED/KILLED, UNTO THE HEBREWS A STUMBLING BLOCK AND UNTO THE GENTILE'S FOOLISHNESS;

Isaiah 2:10-1110. Enter into the rock, and hide thee in the dust, for fear of Yahweh, and for the esteem of his majesty.11. The lofty looks of man shall be humbled, and the haughtiness of men shall be bowed down, and YAHWEH ALONE SHALL BE EXALTED IN THAT DAY.

Revelation 6:15-17

15 Then the kings of the earth, the princes, the generals, the rich, the mighty, and every slave and every free man hid in caves and among the rocks of the mountains. They called to the mountains and the rocks, "Fall on us and

16 And said to the mountains and rocks, fall on us, and HIDE US FROM THE FACE OF HIM WHO SITTETH ON THE THRONE AND FROM THE WRATH OF THE LAMB!

17 FOR THE GREAT DAY OF HIS WRATH HAS COME, AND WHO SHALL STAND?

John 3:36 He that believeth on the Son hath everlasting life: and he that believeth not the Son shall not see life; BUT THE WRATH OF YAHWEH ABIDETH ON HIM.

Revelation 1:8 I AM THE ALPHA AND THE OMEGA," SAYS THE SOVEREIGN YAHWEH, WHO IS AND WHO WAS AND WHO IS TO COME, YAHWEH.

Psalms 83:16-18

16 Fill their faces with shame; THAT THEY MAY SEEK THY NAME, O YAHWEH.

17 Let them be confounded and troubled forever; yea, let them be put to shame, and perish:

18 THAT MEN MAY KNOW THAT THOU, WHOSE NAME ALONE IS YAHWEH, ART THE MOST HIGH OVER ALL THE EARTH.

Malachi 2:16 THEN THEY THAT FEARED YAHWEH SPOKE ONE WITH ANOTHER; AND YAHWEH LISTENED, AND HEARD, AND A BOOK OF REMEMBRANCE WAS WRITTEN BEFORE HIM, FOR THEM THAT FEARED YAHWEH, AND THAT THOUGHT UPON HIS NAME.

Isaiah 43:11 I, EVEN I, AM YAHWEH; AND BESIDE ME THERE IS NO SAVIOR.

Ezekiel 34:23 And I WILL SET UP ONE SHEPHERD OVER THEM, and HE SHALL FEED THEM, even my servant David; HE SHALL FEED THEM, and HE SHALL BE THEIR SHEPHERD.

John 10:3-5

3 To Him the porter openeth; and THE SHEEP HEAR HIS VOICE: and HE CALLETH HIS OWN SHEEP BY NAME, AND LEADETH THEM OUT.

4 And when HE PUTTETH FORTH HIS OWN SHEEP, HE GOETH BEFORE THEM, AND THE SHEEP FOLLOW HIM:

5 And a stranger will they not follow but will flee from him: for they know not the voice of strangers.

Hebrews 4:12,13

12 For the word of Yahweh is quick, and powerful, and sharper than any two edged sword, piercing even to the dividing asunder of soul and spirit, and of the joints and marrow, and is a discerner of the thoughts and intents of the heart.

13 Neither is there any creature that is not manifest in his sight: but all things are naked and opened unto the eyes of him with whom we have to do.

John 8:24,28

24 I said therefore unto you, that ye shall die in your transgressions: for if ye believe not that I am He (YAHWEH), ye shall die in your transgressions.

28 Then said Immanuel unto them, When ye have lifted up the Son of man, then shall ye know that I am He (YAHWEH), and that I do nothing of myself; but as my Father hath taught me, I speak these things.

2 Thessalonians 2:13

But we are bound to give thanks always to Yahweh for you, brethren beloved of Yahweh, because Yahweh hath from the beginning chosen you to salvation through infilling of the Spirit and belief of the truth.

CHAPTER 31
WHAT BELIEVING IN THE SON MEANS

THE BEGINNING TO THE END. READ AND LEARN

NOTE: Many people will use the following verse to try and show that they are saved. But what does this verse really mean?

John 3:16 For Yahweh so loved the world, that he gave his only begotten Son, that whosoever believeth in him should not perish, but have everlasting life.

It is overwhelming at the ignorance that is in the world that people do not even know who the Messiah really is. These scriptures prove who he is and his true name. People need to start opening their minds to what scriptures are really saying instead of what they have been indoctrinated to believe. Do not just read these, study them,

Listen to what they are telling you and receive it with an open mind for you THINK you have eternal life.

John 5:39 Search the scriptures; for in them ye think ye have eternal life: and they are they which testify of me.

Luke 24:44,45

44 And He said to them, these are my words which I spoke to you, while I was yet with you, that all things must be fulfilled, which are written in the law of Moses, and the prophets, and the psalms, concerning me.

45 Then he opened their mind, that they might understand the Scriptures.

John 1:1-5

1 In the beginning was the Word, and the Word WAS WITH Yahweh, and the Word WAS Yahweh.

2 The same was in the beginning with Yahweh.

3 All things were made by him; and without him was not anything made that was made.

4 In him was life; and the life was the light of men.

5 And the light shineth in darkness; and the darkness comprehended it not.

PROVERBS PROVES JOHN

Proverbs 8:22-36

22 YAHWEH POSSESSED ME IN THE BEGINNING OF HIS WAY, BEFORE HIS WORKS OF OLD.

23 I was set up from everlasting, from the beginning, or ever the earth was.

24 When there were no depths, I was brought forth; when there were no fountains abounding with water.

25 Before the mountains were settled, before the hills was I brought forth

26 While as yet He had not made the earth, nor the fields, nor the highest part of the dust of the world.

27 When He prepared the heavens, I was there: when he set a compass upon the face of the depth:

28 When He established the clouds above: when he strengthened the fountains of the deep:

29 When He gave to the sea his decree, that the waters should not pass his commandment: when He appointed the foundations of the earth:

30 Then I was by Him, as one brought up with Him: and I was daily His delight, rejoicing always before Him;

31 Rejoicing in the habitable part of His earth; and my delights were with the sons of men.

32 Now therefore hearken unto Me, O ye children: for blessed are they that keep My ways.

33 Hear instruction, and be wise , and refuse it not.

34 Blessed is the man that heareth Me, watching daily at my gates, waiting at the posts of my doors.

35 For whoso findeth Me findeth life, and shall obtain favor of Yahweh.

36 But He that transgresseth against me wrongeth his own soul: all they that hate Me love death.

John 14:6-29

6 Immanuel saith unto him, I am the way, the truth, and the life: no man cometh unto the Father, but by me.

7 If ye had known me, ye should have known my Father also: and from henceforth ye know Him and have seen Him.

8 Philip told him, "Master, show us the Father, and that will satisfy us."

9 Immanuel saith unto him, Have I been so long time with you, and yet hast thou not known me, Philip? he that hath seen me hath seen the Father; and how sayest thou then, Shew us the Father?

10 Believest thou not that I am in the Father, and the Father in me (SELF SAME SPIRIT)? the words that I speak unto you I speak not of myself: but the Father that dwelleth in me (THE SPIRIT), He doeth the works.

11 Believe me that I am in the Father, and the Father in me: or else believe me for the very works' sake.

12 Verily, verily, I say unto you, He that believeth on me, the works that I do shall he do also; and greater works than these shall he do; because I go unto my Father.

13 And WHATSOEVER YE SHALL ASK IN MY NAME, THAT WILL I DO, that the Father may be esteemed in the Son.

14 IF YE SHALL ASK ANYTHING IN MY NAME, I WILL DO IT.

15 If ye love me, keep my commandments.

16 And I will pray the Father, and he shall give you another Comforter, that he may abide with you forever;

17 Even the Spirit of truth; whom the world cannot receive, because it seeth him not, neither knoweth him: but ye know him; for he dwelleth with you, and shall be in you.

18 I will not leave you comfortless: I will come to you.

19 Yet a little while, and the world seeth me no more; but ye see me: because I live, ye shall live also.

²⁰ At that day ye shall know that I am in my Father, and ye in me, and I in you.

²¹ He that hath my commandments, and keepeth them, he it is that loveth Me: and he that loveth Me shall be loved of my Father, and I will love him, and will manifest myself to him.

²² Judas saith unto him, not Iscariot, Master, how is it that thou wilt manifest thyself unto us, and not unto the world?

²³ Immanuel answered and said unto him, If a man love me, he will keep my words: and my Father will love him, and we will come unto him, and make our abode with him.

²⁴ He that loveth me not keepeth not my sayings: and the word which ye hear is not mine, but the Father's which sent me.

²⁵ These things have I spoken unto you, being yet present with you.

²⁶ But the Comforter, which is the Spirit, whom the Father will send in my name, he shall teach you all things, and bring all things to your remembrance, whatsoever I have said unto you.

²⁷ Peace I leave with you, my peace I give unto you: not as the world giveth, give I unto you. Let not your heart be troubled, neither let it be afraid.

²⁸ Ye have heard how I said unto you, I go away, and come again unto you. If ye loved me, ye would rejoice, because I said, I go unto the Father: for my Father is greater than I.

²⁹ And now I have told you before it come to pass, that, when it is come to pass, ye might believe.

Philippians 2:6 Who, being in the form of Yahweh, thought it not robbery to be equal with Yahweh:

John 8:24,28

24 I said therefore unto you, that ye shall die in your transgressions: for if ye believe not that I am He (YAHWEH), ye shall die in your transgressions.

28 Then said Immanuel unto them, when ye have lifted up the Son of man, then shall ye know that I am He (YAHWEH), and that I do nothing of myself; but as my Father hath taught me, I speak these things.

John 3:18

He that believeth on him is not condemned: but he that believeth not is condemned already, BECAUSE HE HATH NOT BELIEVED IN THE NAME OF THE ONLY BEGOTTEN SON OF YAHWEH.

John 5:43

I AM COME IN MY FATHER'S NAME, and you receive me not, IF ANOTHER SHALL COME IN.

HIS OWN NAME, he ye will receive.

CHAPTER 32
SPIRIT TEACHES

Ephesians 4:6-8, 11-16

6 One Yahweh and Father of all, who is above all, and through all, and in you all.

7 But unto every one of us is given the Spirit according to the measure of the gift of Yahweh.

8 Wherefore he saith, when he ascended up on high, he led captivity captive, and gave gifts unto men.

11 And he gave some, apostles; and some, prophets; [those who speak from Yahweh] and some, evangelists [those who evangelize]; and some, shepherds [those who personally care for the sheep on a one to one basis] and teachers [instruction];

12 For the perfecting of the believers, for the work of the ministry, for the edifying of the body of Yahweh:

13 Till we all come in the unity of the Faith, and of the knowledge of the Son of Yahweh, unto a perfect man, unto the measure of the stature of the fulness of Yahweh:

14 That we henceforth be no more children, tossed to and fro, and carried about with every wind of doctrine, by the sleight of men, and cunning craftiness, whereby they lie in wait to deceive;

15 But speaking the truth in love, may grow up into Him in all things, which is the head, even Yahweh:

16 From whom the whole body fitly joined together and compacted by that which every joint supplieth, according to the effectual working in the measure of every part, maketh increase of the body unto the edifying of itself in love.

Jeremiah 33:3 Call unto me, and I will answer thee, and show thee great and mighty things, which thou knowest not.

Galatians 1:11-12

11 But I (Paul) certify you, brethren, that the truth which was preached/taught of me is not after man.

12 For I neither received it of man neither was I taught it, but by the revelation of Yahweh the Messiah

1 Corinthians 2:4-5

4 And my (PAUL) speech and my preaching/teaching was not with enticing words of man's wisdom, but in demonstration of the Spirit and of power.

5 That your faith should not stand in the wisdom of men, but in the power of Yahweh.

Proverbs 3:5-6

5 Trust in Yahweh with all thine heart; and lean not unto thine own understanding.

6 In all thy ways acknowledge him, and he shall direct thy paths.

Psalms 32:8 I will instruct thee and teach thee in the way which thou shalt go: I will guide thee with mine eye.

Psalms 25:9 The meek will He guide in judgment: and the meek will He teach his way.

1 John 2:20, 27

[20] But ye have an unction from the Righteous One, and you know all things.

[27] But the anointing which ye have received of Him abideth in you, and ye need not that any man teach you: But as the same anointing teacheth you all things, and is truth, and is not lie, and even as it has taught you, ye shall abide in Him.

John 14:26 But the Comforter, which is the Spirit, whom the Father will send in my name, he shall teach you all things, and bring all things to your remembrance, whatsoever I have said unto you.

John 16:13 Howbeit when He, the Spirit of truth is come, He will guide you into all truths: for He will not speak of Himself; but whatsoever He should hear, that shall He speak: and He will show you things to come.

Once people are given Yahweh's Latter-Day Spirit for those who believe at that time, they will need no man to teach them, just like those from Pentecost to the last Roman Emperor Persecution.

CHAPTER 33
THE UNPARDONABLE
TRANSGRESSION

Hebrews 6:4-6

4 For it is impossible for those who were once enlightened, and have tasted of the heavenly gift, and were made partakers of the Spirit,

5 And have tasted the good Word of Yahweh, and the powers of the world to come,

6 If they shall fall away, to renew them again unto repentance; seeing they crucify to themselves the Son of Yahweh afresh and put him to an open shame.

Matthew 12:31-32

31 Wherefore I say unto you, ALL manner of transgression and blasphemy shall be forgiven unto man: but the blasphemy against the Spirit shall not be forgiven unto man.

32 And whosoever speaketh a word against the Son of man, it shall be forgiven him: but whosoever speaketh against the Spirit, it shall not be forgiven him, neither in this world, neither in the world to come.

WHO IS THE SPIRIT? YAHWEH.

The unpardonable transgression, which is blasphemy of the Spirit, is being filled with Yahweh's Spirit and then turning your back on Him. At that time, there is no more forgiveness for you. So, only a true believer can commit this unpardonable act.

1 John 5:9-20

9 If we receive the witness of men, the witness of Yahweh is greater: for this is the witness of Yahweh which He hath testified of his Son.

10 He that believeth on the Son of Yahweh hath the witness in himself: he that believeth not Yahweh hath made him a liar; because he believeth not the record that Yahweh gave of his Son.

11 And this is the record, that Yahweh hath given to us eternal life, and this life is in his Son.

12 He that hath the Son hath life; and he that hath not the Son of Yahweh hath not life.

Acts 2:33 Therefore being by the right hand of Yahweh exalted, and having received of the Father the promise of the Spirit, he hath shed forth this, which ye now see and hear.

Galatians 4:6 And because ye are sons, Yahweh hath sent forth the Spirit of his Son into your hearts, crying, Abba, Father.

13 These things have I written unto you that believe on the name of the Son of Yahweh; that ye may know that ye have eternal life, and that ye may believe on the name of the Son of Yahweh.

14 And this is the confidence that we have in Him, that, if we ask any thing according to his will, He heareth us:

15 And if we know that He hear us, whatsoever we ask, we know that we have the petitions that we desired of Him.

16 If any man see his brother transgress a transgression which is not unto death, he shall ask, and He shall give him life for them that transgress not unto death. There is a transgression unto death: I do not say that he shall pray for it.

17 All unrighteousness is transgression: and there is a transgression not unto death.

18 *We know that whosoever is born of Yahweh transgresseth not; but he that is begotten of Yahweh keepeth himself, and that wicked one toucheth him not.*

19 And we know that we are of Yahweh, and the whole world lieth in wickedness.

20 And we know that the Son of Yahweh is come, and hath given us an understanding, that we may know him that is true, and we are in him that is true, even in his Son Yahweh Messiah. This is the true Yahweh, and eternal life.